THE <u>NEW</u> HONEY REVOLUTION

*Restoring the Health of
Future Generations*

(REVISED AND UPDATED)

RON FESSENDEN, MD, MPH

TGBTGBooks.com, LLC
Colorado Springs, Colorado

CONTENTS

FOREWORD

"The words of wise men are like goads, and masters of these collections are like well-driven nails; they are given by one Shepherd. But beyond this, my son, be warned: the writing of many books is endless, and excessive devotion to books is wearying to the body." (Ecclesiastes 12: 11-12, New American Standard Version)

This Truth is unchanging. Yet such is not always the case for many other established truths, especially in the realm of medical knowledge. The reader's forbearance is humbly requested. Since the first edition of **The Honey Revolution – Restoring the Health of Future Generations** (2008), and **The Honey Revolution – Abridged** (2010), were published, new information has been discovered and confirmed by research. Rather than simply reprint previously published titles, it was reasoned that a revised and updated book might be appropriate, incorporating not only the relevant information from those books, but also the new information.

The intention for this revised and updated version is to summarize and condense what is known today about the health benefits of honey in one easy to read edition. In five or six years, as more is known (which is a certainty given the exploding interest in honey research today[1]) perhaps there will have to be another updated and revised edition consistent with the Truth above that the "writing of many books is endless . . ."

Much of what is contained in this new edition is taken directly from previous books in *The Honey Revolution* series. However, content has been reorganized in a more logical and hopefully more readable fashion. References left out of the *Abridged* version of *The Honey Revolution* have been provided where indicated and new research cited where applicable. Material from *Feed Your Brain First* (2013) has been included as it represents the most relevant information available regarding how honey differs from other sugars, and most importantly, why honey fuels the brain first, while the consumption of other sugars contributes to brain starvation.

None of the books in *The Honey Revolution* series (which now totals four books[2] including this book) would have been possible without the collaboration and brilliance of Mike McInnes, MRPS of Edinburgh, Scotland, my co-author for the first two books, and to him I am grateful for starting me on this journey of discovery and knowledge.

INTRODUCTION

This book is about honey–a wonderful, miraculous, natural food. It is not a diet book. It is a book about how regular consumption of honey will reduce your risks for many diseases and medical conditions, help you sleep better, improve your immune system functions, and help you experience better health as you age.

This is a revolutionary book. Revolutions are spawned out of extreme circumstances and profound need. If there was ever a time for a dietary revolution, it is now. We have a problem in America. The problem is a weighty one. Roughly two-thirds of us are overweight or obese. Nearly 20% of children under the age of 18 are medically obese. Estimates are that by 2030, 86% of our population will be obese. Obesity and being overweight have been shown to increase the risk for developing type 2 diabetes, heart disease, some forms of cancer, and other disabling medical conditions. Over 24 million (nearly 10% of the population) are diagnosed with diabetes and a staggering 57 million people are pre-diabetic. Over 100,000 individuals die each year from obesity related cancers. This public health time bomb is ticking.

There is another aspect to a revolution that motivates the writing of this book. This involves a change of thinking described in the first chapter. We need to change the way we think about honey. This book is written to dispel ignorance on the part of both the consuming public and healthcare professionals and nutritionists who continue to believe that honey is just sugar, and all sugars are the same. This may prove to be a formidable task given the comments that continue to appear in print in reputable newspapers, magazines and various association publications – comments that would lead us to believe that sugar, whether from cane, beets, corn, or honey is all the same, digested, stored, and metabolized within the body in the same way.

The problem is complex; however, the answers are surprisingly simple. To adopt (and modify) a phrase from a well-known political campaign of the 1990s, "It's the sugar, stupid." That is why the first third of this book may appear to be chasing rabbits down tortuous trails, discussing sugars and artificial sweeteners, and "standards of identity" for honey. It may make for a slow start, but, once you understand the differences between honey and other sugars or artificial sweeteners, and the need to have a honey standard, the exciting facts about the health benefits of honey that follow will have a firm foundation and increased credibility.

The state of scientific research relating to honey, as a healthful food, is incomplete as of mid 2014 just as it was when the first iteration of this book was written in 2008. Many of the studies cited in the first edition of *The Honey Revolution* were small observational studies using animals and/or humans with fewer than 50 test subjects. Though the findings then were preliminary, they were very promising. The same is true today. However, the weight of scientific evidence confirming the powerful health benefits of honey is growing. New potential benefits to consuming this amazing food, such as enhancements to the immune system and positive effects in preventing or fighting cancer are not only revolutionary but also amazing and are spawning more research, even as we write.

It may be that research studies comparing the health benefits of honey to other sugars using large populations may never be completed. The reasons for this are quite simple. Honey is a "non-standardized" food with over 300 varietals produced in the United States and Canada alone. Results produced by the consumption of one varietal may not be the same as those from another. And no research or study design would include a comparison of 300 varietals. Then there is the economic interest (or lack of it) from researching a potential health benefit from a natural product for which there is little profit incentive for the research sponsor. Finally, randomized, controlled research or studies based on retrospective observations are difficult, if not impossible, to conduct given the fact that populations not exposed to sugar or high fructose corn syrup (HFCS) needed to serve as controls would be hard to find.

The refined sugar, HFCS, and processed food industries are quick to respond to any research and published reports that indict their products. They point out that a causal relationship has not been proven between sugar, fructose and/or HFCS consumption and the host of medical conditions that have been increasing in incidence over the past 40 years. They are technically correct. Retrospective studies that have shown significant association between high consumption of sucrose and/or HFCS and the increasing incidence of metabolic diseases *are not designed to prove causality*. Statistically, they cannot *prove* anything. They can only show significance or strength of association. The same is true of prospective and/or observational studies. Unfortunately, too many medical professionals, nutritionists, and public agency spokespersons have ignored common sense, insisting only on "proof" while strong associations between dietary trends and increasing prevalence of disease continue to attack our public health.

So what about honey? If you persevere through the first third of this book, you will be convinced that honey is one possible solution to the public health challenge facing America. Honey may also be the solution for health challenges that you may be facing. Honey is certainly not part of the problem.

The chapter entitled "Honey: Nature's Amazing Medicine" and the chapters following describe *five categories of health benefits* derived from honey. It is not to be assumed that these categories are distinct or unique, for as you will see, there is considerable overlap among the mechanisms of action within these sections, especially among the sections describing the metabolic benefits of consuming honey, the benefits of honey for sleep, and the effects of honey on the immune system.

Honey is curative but it is not a cure-all. Honey consumption can reverse some of the indicators for diabetes. It can lower blood sugar and HbA_{1c} levels, but only over time. It can help lower triglycerides and total cholesterol. It will enhance immune system functioning. Honey will facilitate and ensure restorative sleep. However, honey cannot fix decades of abusive dietary habits. To a generation of folks who have come to demand cures over prevention, the suggestion to substitute honey for sugar or HFCS, is likely to be ignored by those needing immediate gratification and results. For some, this suggestion will be too late.

Honey is preventative. It is not too late for a generation of children who need desperately to change eating habits and eliminate the excessive quantities of refined sugar and HFCS from their diets and begin using honey. It is not too late for millions of younger and middle-aged adults to do the same and reduce their risks for a number of metabolic diseases.

Shifting momentum and changing direction in a vast dietary ocean with many competing forces at work on the "ship of public health" will not be easy. Though the principles presented in this book are simple, their application over time faces many challenges, not the least of which will be from our federal agencies and professional organizations whose recommendations and support of misguided dietary guidelines have led us to this crisis, the processed food industry whose millions of dollars of profits are at stake, the medical institutions whose research dollars and double-blinded studies have produced spurious and confounding results, and the medical professionals, nutritionists, and dietitians whose advice regarding carbohydrates and fats has done little to stem the advance of obesity, diabetes, cardiovascular disease and other metabolic stress related conditions.

Recently I had the opportunity to spend about 30 minutes discussing the principles of this book with a curious high school teacher. She suffered from a few of the conditions described in the book. As she began to grasp the truth that by proper fueling of the liver with honey throughout the day and at bedtime she could reduce metabolic stress, her interest peaked. Realizing that she could reverse, over time, the consequences of years of self-destructive eating behaviors, she finally exclaimed, "Why haven't we been taught these things before? Why hasn't my doctor told me about this?"

The knowledge of honey metabolism and its application to the human system are emerging as powerful tools with which to fight disease. Honey, and its ability to optimize glucose metabolism and therefore influence and control fat metabolism, as compared to all other refined sugars or sweeteners, may be ignored by the various health professions. Equally overlooked is the principle of fueling the liver with honey before bedtime, and how that may affect sleep and recovery physiology. Yet increasingly, the consumption of honey is being found to have positive impact on all the chronic adrenal-driven diseases, heart disease, hypertension, type 2 diabetes, obesity, osteoporosis, gastric ulcers, infertility, depression, memory loss and dementias.

One timeless truth prevails: *"Eat honey, my son, for it is good . . ." (Proverbs 24:13, New International Version)*

NOTE TO THE READER

A casual reading of the table of contents or a brief perusal of this book or others in *The Honey Revolution Series* might lead you to believe that honey is being presented as a "cure" for many diseases and conditions. Such is not the case. You should be skeptical of such broad cure-all claims made for any natural food product, including honey. Honey is a healthful food to be sure, but it cannot, in all cases, reverse what months and years of dietary indiscretions, lifestyle choices, and/or genetics have caused.

The benefits of honey for many of life's ailments described in multiple sections of this book are repetitious. This is intended; however, the fact that honey works for many conditions in various ways should not be ignored in spite of the repetition. Regular honey consumption at bedtime will result in improved sleep patterns and reduced nighttime metabolic stress almost immediately for most individuals. Honey will regulate your blood sugar, lower your cholesterol, help with memory and cognition, and much more. Not everyone will read this book from cover to cover. Many, perhaps most of you, will jump to the section or sections more applicable for you. By doing this, you will avoid what may be viewed by some as unnecessary redundancy. If you do persevere throughout every page, it is my hope that you see honey as truly a remarkable food, bringing benefit to many across a wide range of health conditions in a diverse number of ways.

The information provided in this book is not intended to be a substitute for the advice and counsel of your personal physician. Suggestions regarding the use of honey are recommendations, not prescriptions or medical guidelines for self-treatment and should not be substituted for any treatment recommendations prescribed by your physician. While the recommendations are appropriate and risk free for most people, individuals have differing requirements and/or responses to dietary recommendations based on their complete medical profile. Many disease processes as well as their ultimate prognoses may be irreversible. You should also note that reductions in risks for any disease or condition are determined across large populations and do not necessarily apply to each individual within that population.

Finally, throughout the pages of this book, short stories of real people are included. Some of these stories appear in other books in *The Honey Revolution Series* and have been adapted for use here. These stories are told as one individual's experience, but the story is often representative of multiple individuals, all sharing similar facts. Some of these stories underscore how lifestyle and dietary habits have negatively impacted health. Others relate how willingness to go against conventional wisdom and adopt a seemingly counterintuitive dietary strategy can result in better health. You can become one of those in this latter group by joining *the honey revolution*.

THE HONEY REVOLUTION: CHANGING THE WAY WE THINK ABOUT HONEY

"Eat honey, my son, for it is good . . ." (Proverbs 24:13, New International Version)

Webster's Online Dictionary defines *revolution* as "a fundamental change in the way of thinking about or visualizing something: a change of paradigm . . ." That is exactly why **The Honey Revolution** books were written – to change the way you think about honey.

As a physician, it is most disconcerting to hear other physicians state that "honey is just sugar" or to hear patients report that their physician or nutrition counselor told them that honey is just another sugar and must be avoided or limited, especially in those with some degree of glucose intolerance.

Honey is a combination of two sugars, glucose and fructose in nearly equal parts. In addition, honey contains small amounts of other compound sugars[3] and over 180 other substances not found in HFCS or table sugar (sucrose). These are part of the reasons why honey is metabolized in the human system differently than other sugars such as HFCS or table sugar, sugars which are also made up of equal or nearly equal parts of glucose and fructose.

This miraculous food is often referred to as "nature's sweetener," but categorizing honey as a sweetener communicates a lesser truth about honey. Beyond its sweetness, honey is a natural food that contains many health-promoting properties. It is a super food, a gold standard of carbohydrates, and a revolutionary food, bringing many health benefits to those who consume it regularly.

It all starts with discovering the origins of this sweet natural food given to us by the Creator. The process of creating honey begins as photons from the sun stimulate photosynthesis by bombarding chloroplasts in plants. These plants then mature, flower, and produce nectar, a sweet combination of sucrose and glucose in differing ratios.

The honeybee gathers nectar from a diversity of floral sources, preferring nectar that contains a mixture of glucose and sucrose rather than one predominating in either sugar. Enzymes in the honeybee's honey sac (a specialized collecting chamber in the bee for storage of foraged nectar) degrade or split the sucrose into fructose and glucose, producing a blend containing a nearly equal ratio of both sugars — nature's perfect ratio required for the formation of liver glycogen, which is the primary fuel for the brain. This conversion of sucrose to glucose and fructose by the honeybee comes at a high-energy toll, a fact that argues against some chance occurrence or metabolic accident and argues for intentional design by the Creator. It was clearly in the Creator's plan to provide us with this wonderful, miraculous food.

As nectar in the honey sac is combined with enzymes from the honeybee and returned to the hive, it is passed from one honeybee to another, sometimes involving several hand-offs from bee to bee, each one adding more enzymes that serve to dilute and ripen the nectar into honey. Once the mixture is placed in the comb cells, other honeybees fan the nectar with their wings, sometimes for several hours to dehydrate the honey until it reaches an average moisture content of between 18 and 20%. Though pollen has been carefully removed from the nectar during its collection and transport to the hive, pollen is added back to the ripening honey by the honeybee before the honey cells are capped and sealed for more ripening and storage in the comb.

Honey Processing

The methods of removing honey from the hive, extracting it from the frames holding the wax comb, straining it, and packing it in containers for personal consumption or to sell varies widely among honey producers. The hobbyist beekeeper who maintains only a few hives may extract honey manually, removing the frames of comb from the hive, shaving off the wax caps, and spinning out the honey in a small hand operated extractor (a centrifuge that rotates the frames and spins out the honey). The honey may be run through a fine pore sieve or metal filter to remove large particles, wax, and other material that has found its way into the honey during its removal from the frames before collecting it in buckets or barrels for storage. Sometimes the honey is warmed slightly to temperatures that do not exceed 110°F to make the process of straining and filling small containers easier.

Commercial honey producers may keep several hundred to several thousand hives. For these large producers, honey extraction is highly mechanized. Hives, or "supers" as they are called, are collected from multiple bee yards and brought to an extracting facility or "honey house." These supers hold several frames of comb, each filled with honey (the honeybees and their brood are left behind in the bee yard to continue the process of raising more honeybees and producing more honey). Mechanized automated processors uncap the comb, place the frames in giant extractors and spin out the honey, which is then collected, run through a sieve and pumped into large tanks. From there, the honey is pumped into 55-gallon drums, sealed and stored until sold or needed for the next step in processing. Depending on the ambient temperature, the moisture content of the honey, the particular varietal, and length of time kept in the drums until the honey is processed and packed, the honey will crystallize and become almost solid. Honey will keep indefinitely in sealed drums and will not spoil. Some commercial honey producers maintain millions of pounds of honey in storage from year to year.

Honey is packed and sold under a variety of labels. It is important to understand the processes used in packing honey as many of the health benefits of consuming honey can be affected by how it is processed and sold. Understanding leads to making informed choices. The health benefits of honey also vary depending on the specific varietal so it is important to choose wisely. Only pure, unadulterated, unfiltered honey will provide optimum health benefits.[4]

If you are just discovering honey or starting to use it for health reasons, you may be a bit curious about the varieties and brands of honey available in the market. Which honey is best? What kind of honey provides the most health benefits? Is there an advantage to local honey?

Along with answering these questions, let's first define a few terms that apply to honey, as it is sold or available today.

Honey Varietals

Honey, like wine, can be purchased in multiple floral and taste variations. Most of the honey consumed in the U.S. is from a combination of several unidentified floral nectar sources. This honey may be labeled as "clover honey" and may also contain honey from other floral nectars.

When you venture away from the routine and try different honey varietals, you quickly discover their amazing qualities and taste sensations.

Some varietals can only be found in health food stores, specialty kitchen shops, or online, but the effort to find them will be worth it. Orange blossom, lavender, eucalyptus, Tupelo, Kiawe, or even wild flower honey from the western slopes of Colorado will become personal favorites.

By the same process, however, some honey varietals, like raw unfiltered coffee flower honey from the highlands of Chiapas, Mexico may be left to crystallize on the pantry shelf. It just doesn't taste good! Perhaps it has healthful benefits that compensate for its taste.

Honey Varietals and Health Benefits

Different honey varietals may offer specific health benefits. As examples: darker honeys have been found to possess higher concentrations of antioxidants; buckwheat honey is an inexpensive and efficient cough suppressant, proven to be more effective than the most familiar over-the-counter cough suppressant;[5] Manuka honey possesses powerful antibiotic characteristics.

Additional research is underway in many countries around the world. Hundreds of studies have been conducted within the past few years that document the health benefits of many honey varietals, their active ingredients, and the physiologic mechanisms by which they work within the human system. Dozens of published articles can be found covering topics that include: honey and cough, honey and wound healing, honey as an antibacterial agent, honey and Helicobacter,[6] honey and cancer, and honey as a dermatological treatment. Most all of these research studies use an identified honey varietal. Some studies compare several varietals in their effectiveness against a particular condition. Later in this book, specific conditions and diseases will be discussed along with honey varietals that have been shown to have therapeutic effects for those diseases.

Honey Terms

Raw honey is pure honey as it comes directly from the hive. It has not been diluted, heated or combined with diatomaceous earth and filtered through micropore filters. Nothing has been added or removed.

Comb honey is honey that is packed with a portion of the comb included. The wax comb from the frame in the hive is cut into pieces and packed into tubs or jars with honey. Destroying the comb in this way by making it unavailable for reuse by the bees increases the cost to the consumer. Some comb honey is actually produced directly by the honeybees in the small 6 or 8-ounce tub-sized portions in which it is sold. The small empty containers are placed in the hive within a frame. Honeybees create new comb within the small tubs and fill it with honey. This method of producing comb honey is nature's way of automating production. Those folks who prefer comb honey, however, should be aware that it is possible for herbicides and pesticides, to which honeybees may become exposed while foraging for nectar and pollen, can accumulate within the wax comb over time.

Granulated or crystallized honey is thick, almost solid honey in which the sugars have become crystallized naturally over time. Most honey varietals will crystallize eventually given normal conditions.[7, 8] This honey has not turned bad and need not be discarded. It is easy to re-liquefy crystallized honey by placing the honey container in a warm water bath not exceeding 110°F for a period of time until the honey returns to its liquid state.

Spun honey, or creamed honey as it is sometimes called, is honey that has been artificially crystallized and spun or whipped until reaching a uniform spreadable consistency. The processing of spun honey requires that liquid honey first be heated slightly to dissolve any larger crystals that may be present. Then smaller seed crystals are added, and the honey is spun or whipped until it is crystallized evenly throughout the batch. Fruit or other flavors may be added to the honey to produce flavored spun honey. The pre-crystallized honey is then placed in plastic or glass containers and labeled.

In Europe, spun honey is preferred by most of the honey consuming public. The shelf life is longer since the honey is already crystallized and, if kept in a cooler environment, will not liquefy.

Blended honey refers to honey from multiple sources that has been mixed together prior to bottling or packing. Blended honey may come from several domestic sources or be imported from various countries. It is not required that labels indicate that honey has been blended from multiple sources, nor is a Country of Origin statement required. Hence, honey that is packed or bottled by several of the large honey packing companies and resold as generic U.S. Grade A Honey may be honey from many sources and more than one country.

Pure honey is simply that – natural honey with nothing added or removed. However, it is not the intent here to perpetuate the myth that honey dwells in a realm of ultra purity. All pure honey will contain trace amounts of foreign substances and/or contaminants. These trace substances may include residues of pesticides, antibiotics, anti-mite chemicals, or other substances that the honeybee may come into contact with while gathering nectar and pollen. As there currently are no requirements for testing for contaminants in honey in the U.S., information regarding trace amounts of these substances that may or may not be found in honey are not readily available.

Organic honey may be purchased in the U.S. but most, if not all of it, is imported honey. Honeybees will fly up to three miles to gather nectar and there are few areas in the U.S. where nectar-producing blossoms exist that are not exposed to agricultural or industrial chemicals. Organic honey is available from Brazil. However, when purchasing organic honey, keep in mind that the certification processes for organic foods may differ from country to country.

U.S. Grade A Honey is found on the labels of many honey brands and varietals. This label is somewhat misleading, as there are no mandatory grading *requirements* for honey packed or sold in the U.S. Grading Standards do exist and have been published by the USDA, but they are *voluntary standards* and serve as a basis for inspection and grading by the Federal inspection service.

Heating honey is required in the packing or bottling of honey to decrease its viscosity and allow it to pass through filters or sieves to remove contaminants. Most honey packers heat honey from 140° to 160°F to dissolve any crystals and lengthen its shelf life. Heating honey above 160°F for a lengthy period of time will change the character and color of honey. Heating honey also increases the amount of methylglyoxal (MGO) that it contains, and may degrade some of its enzymes more rapidly.

Strained honey refers to honey that has been run through a fine pore metal sieve to remove wax or other particulate matter that may be present. Strained honey is an official type of extracted honey as defined in the USDA Grading Standards. Strained honey has no component specifying clarity.

Filtered honey is another official type of extracted honey as defined by the USDA Grading Standards. The process of filtering honey is facilitated by the addition of diatomaceous earth (DE), a process used by most large honey packers. Diatomaceous earth consists of fossilized remains of a type of hard-shelled algae (diatoms). The powdery DE acts as an absorbent removing ultra fine particles that may be found in the honey. The process involves adding DE to the honey, heating it and then filtering it through a series of fine micro-filters to remove all micro-contaminants including most of the DE. Most of the beneficial pollen residues naturally contained in honey are also removed by filtering with DE.

Most small honey packers or honey producers that pack their own honey for sale at local markets do not filter honey. Honey sold in retail stores and labeled as "unfiltered" indicates that the honey has only been strained and not filtered with DE before packing. Unfiltered honey will crystallize or granulate sooner than DE filtered honey. If this happens, simply heat the honey container in a warm water bath (110°F) until it returns to a liquid state. It is not recommended that a microwave be used to heat honey.

Tolerance Limits for Contaminants in Honey

Honeybees are fragile insects. It is the responsibility of the beekeeper to tend his bees in such a way as to promote their healthy state. Throughout the year, honeybees will need treatment with chemicals to prevent mite infestations. Antibiotics may need to be applied for bacterial infections that can occur in and destroy a hive. As a result, trace levels of these chemicals and antibiotics may be present in honey. These are not harmful to humans at the levels (usually in fractions of a part per million) found in honey.

These trace levels need not unnecessarily concern honey consumers for this reason. The amount of honey an individual consumes daily is typically a very small amount. Even when ingested in the amounts suggested in parts of this book, the daily dose of honey consumed is not such that trace contaminants would cause harm. These statements are not meant to excuse or rationalize the presence of trace contaminants in honey. Rather they are meant to encourage the adoption of reasonable tolerance limits based on good science.

THE CASE FOR A HONEY STANDARD

"God cares about honesty in the workplace; your business is his business." (Proverbs 16:11, The Message)

It is perhaps an absurd reality in an age where product information is as close as a Google search, product knowledge proliferates at the speed of Facebook, and regulatory requirements mandate truth-in-labeling for almost everything, that you can purchase and consume something, anything, and not be confident that what it says on the label is what is really in the container. Yet, that does not seem to be the case where honey is concerned.

The word honey appears in the ingredients list for everything from biscuits and bread and baklava to cereal and crackers and cakes on one end of the alphabet all the way to yogurt at the other. Whether sold as a stand-alone product or added to processed foods or used in baked goods, honey is not always honey, or at least not honey as defined by some standard. In reality, there is no standard, except in six States.

You can open packets labeled "honey sauce" in fast food restaurants or purchase honey-glazed ham for that special occasion being confident of one thing – what is being called honey may not be honey at all, and if it does actually turn out to be honey, the source of that honey cannot be determined. Honey used in baked goods and other processed foods is typically a product known as "baker's blend" or "industrial honey" – a completely legal product in the U.S. that is only 49% honey at best – a product that costs less than half the cost of raw honey to produce. When you buy honey in a container conspicuously labeled U.S. Grade A Pure Honey, there is still reason to doubt the veracity of the label and its contents.

This confusion can only be blamed on one fact. There is no accepted "Standard of Identity" for honey in the U.S. Even those within the industry (beekeepers, honey producers, importers, packers, and even the National Honey Board) cannot agree on what honey is. Furthermore, members of those groups, who have every reason to know better, are fiercely divided as to whether such a standard is needed and if so, what that should be.

Not only is honey undefined by any uniform standard, most American consumers seem to accept that honey is a commodity that may or may not be simply honey. Of those individuals surveyed in a 2006 study conducted by the National Honey Board and repeated in 2009, most believed that other ingredients are added to honey, including "various syrups, sugars and/or preservatives."

The History and Current Status of Honey Standards

How this confusion about honey came to be is an important part of the story, just as important as any discussion of a honey standard itself. For decades, even centuries, honey was honey, a pure sweet substance produced by honeybees. Ancient civilizations revered honey, sought diligently for it, memorialized it in poems and songs, wrote about it in sacred literature, and considered it useful in ceremony and religious rites.

As early as 1878, the issue was brought to the attention of the U.S. Senate and Congress when a petition was presented to prohibit the adulteration and sale of honey and other natural sweeteners with glucose. Yet it was not until 1968 that the U.S., along with the Food and Agricultural Organization of the United Nations and the World Health Organization produced a "Draft Provisional Standard for Honey" in which the definition and description of honey (an international honey standard, if you will) was agreed upon as follows:

"Honey means exclusively the sweet substance produced by honey bees from the nectar of blossoms or from secretions of or on living parts of plants, which they collect, transform and combine with specific substances, and store in honey combs.

Honey consists essentially of a concentrated solution of different sugars, predominately glucose and fructose. Besides glucose and fructose, honey contains protein, amino acids, enzymes, organic acids, mineral substances, pollen and other substances, and may include sucrose, maltose, melezitose and other oligosaccharides (including dextrins) as well as traces of fungi, algae, yeasts, and other solid particles resulting from the process of obtaining honey . . ."

Several countries, including many from the European Economic Community, Latin America, the United States, Australia and New Zealand used this draft, and other efforts that preceded it, to adopt similar honey standards' legislation. Arthur Fasler summarizes these "standards" in a chapter in Eva Crane's book *Honey A Comprehensive Survey*.[9] Essentially these standards were in agreement with the general definition and description of honey given above. What is striking about these preliminary standards are the elements they have in common and the assumptions left unstated. For example, most permitted the importation of honey and the blending of honey from other countries, *as long as* the Country of Origin and the percentages from each were clearly stated on the label. Most called for *identification of the supplier* on the label, including specifically the name and address of that supplier. All of *these preliminary standards assumed that pollen was an essential component of honey*. In other words, there were no references made to the amount or percentage of pollen content or conversely, references indicating the lack of it. Most standards had prohibitions for what was called "artificial honey." If artificial honey was permitted, required labeling declarations were specific as to the list of ingredients that must be included.

The first international standard for honey was formally adopted by the Codex Alimentarius Commission in 1987, and a Revised Codex Standard was similarly adopted in 2001. The United States participated fully in these and earlier proceedings. However, as of the present date, there is no official standard of identity for honey in U.S. law. In 2006, and again in 2011, the American Beekeeping Federation, Inc., the American Honey Producers Association, Inc., the National Honey Packers and Dealers Association, the Sioux Honey Association and the Western States Packers and Dealers Association formally petitioned the United States DHHS Food and Drug Administration (FDA) to formally adopt certain provisions of the 2001 Revised Codex Standard for Honey into law.

This petition was rejected on both occasions concluding that the petition did not provide reasonable grounds for the FDA to adopt the Codex Standard for Honey. Furthermore, the rejection notification concluded that the agency's existing enforcement tools are sufficient to address the concerns of the petition and "the establishment of a standard of identity would not aid the agency in its enforcement efforts or help insure industry compliance." This last statement might be credible if it were not for the complete lack of logic assumed in such a pronouncement. How can there be enforcement or industry compliance in the absence of a standard? On what basis can anyone or any agency enforce anything if there is no accepted definition of what that anything is? Not only does it defy logic, it defies common sense.

Astonishing, as it may seem, there would still be no official standard of identity for honey in any of the States if it were not for the tireless efforts of one individual. About six years ago, Nancy Gentry, a beekeeper from Florida, began work that resulted in a standard of identity being adopted for honey in the State of Florida. The Florida Standard was codified under the rulemaking authority of the Legislature, rather than by the passage of new legislation on July 14, 2009.

Perhaps some of the blame for the U.S. not having a Federal Standard can be leveled at the honey industry itself. The National Honey Board, which is in reality a packer/importer board, cannot insert itself in the regulatory process or influence legislation, except by educating the public. At present, the NHB is content to state on its official website "Honey that is filtered through more traditional methods is still 'honey,' even if pollen has been removed along with other fine particles." Others in the industry would disagree, stating that if all pollen has been removed from honey, one cannot prove with certainty that the product is honey. Country of origin certainly cannot be proven.[10]

State standards, as mentioned, are relatively new, as efforts to codify into State laws a Standard of Identity for honey have only been in process for a few years, thanks to Nancy Gentry's original work in Florida. Though twenty-four states are known to be in the process of adopting a honey standard, the initiative seems to have been stalled perhaps due to the litigation emerging in several States that do have a Standard of Identity for honey.

One State, North Carolina, has in place a voluntary honey standard that was initiated through the efforts of the state's active beekeeper association, honey producers and state regulators. Though voluntary, the standard does apply to all honey sold at state sponsored markets. Testing of honey sold in these markets is required and funded by assessments paid by the honey producer and the state association. This type of standard has seemed to work well in North Carolina but has little application in other States, which do not have state-sponsored sales outlets for honey.

Among honey producers there is little agreement regarding a definition and description of honey, and for perhaps good reasons. One beekeeper known to the author, who produces the finest certifiable organic honey in the world, is opposed to a standard because it would potentially impact his export of honey to certain countries. The reason, his honey – though delicious and without doubt pure honey – is produced from nectar from the Kiawe tree flower. Through no fault of his own and certainly through no fault of the honeybees, this honey, at various times of the year, contains higher sucrose content than the 10–15% sucrose typically allowed in most honey composition standards. Countries which test honey imports have not allowed his honey to be imported because of this higher than usual sucrose content, believing that sucrose has been added to honey.

Other standards in existence would seem to implicate and limit the sale or import of honey due to factors beyond the control of packers or honey producers, including several completely normal situations that occur with honey. Standards that include strict levels of hydroxymethylfurfural (HMF) and methylglyoxal (MGO) serve as good examples. HMF was originally thought not to be a constituent of honey and thus its presence was considered evidence of prolonged storage, overheating or addition of sugars to honey. However, hundreds of studies conducted over the last century have shown that small amounts of HMF are found in unprocessed honey. Adding to the confusion over HMF content in honey is the fact that standards vary widely from country to country.

The same is true of MGO. While MGO is not found in most honey, some varietals such as Manuka honey from nectar from the leptospermum flower found in Australia and New Zealand contain over 1000 times the concentration of MGO than other honey varietals. Testing that shows higher levels of MGO in honey is also believed by some to be an evidence of overheating of honey, yet it is a natural constituent of some honey varietals as indicated.

Opposition to a Honey Standard

From Honey Packers and Importers. It is with some irony that we note again that as recent as early 2011, honey packers and importers, as represented by the National Honey Packers and Dealers Association and the Western States Packers and Dealers Association sponsored, along with other groups, a petition to the FDA to adopt certain provisions of the Revised Codex Standard as revised in 2001. Among the provisions that were recommended to be included were the sections that defined and described honey as quoted earlier. What a difference a few months and a dozen lawsuits have made to the unified support for an international honey standard as evidenced by what follows.

At a meeting described as a "Roundtable" convened for discussion and consideration of a "Revised Standard of Identity for Honey" held in Las Vegas on May 16, 2012, recommendations adopted by the group seemed to suggest that a honey standard should permit the import, packing, or sale of products called "honey" to which *anything* could have been added OR from which any essential constituent had been removed. In addition, other recommendations insisted that all labeling requirements be removed as they might apply to importers, packers, and resellers of honey.[11] Such disregard for product integrity and truth in labeling seems to be incredulous.

Packers, who buy honey from many sources, including importers, may resist standards, as they seemingly have no control over the quality standards that may or may not exist for the products they purchase for resale. Many standards are obscure or conflicting and inconsistently applied and regulated. Packers blend honey to achieve proper color or consistency of flavor or sugar ratios for obvious reasons. Most large commercial packers process honey by micro filtering to improve shelf life and salability of the product. For reasons known only to individual packers, however, there is a hesitancy to label honey that is packed and sold to retail outlets accurately and truthfully.

In their defense, no individual or company welcomes the risk of product liability or truth-in-labeling lawsuits. And no one anticipated the litigious fallout from the passage of seemingly innocuous honey standards that have become law in six States. Furthermore, packers and importers of honey may justifiably oppose a honey standard, which holds them liable for something not in their control, such as fraud, misrepresentation, mislabeling, circumvention of customs, or even product quality on the part of those who would sell honey to them.

Another logical defense for packers in opposing a strict standard for honey is motivated by customer demand and expectations. In the "Use and Attitude Survey" conducted periodically by the National Honey Board, a majority of respondents indicated a preference for "light, clear" honey, free from any visible particulate matter. American consumers are particularly hesitant to buy honey in which crystallization has begun or is visible to any degree, believing that the honey has "gone bad" or "turned to sugar." "It's what the customer prefers," seems to be the major driver for the typical processing methods used by most large packers. Some retailers and wholesale resellers of honey demand that honey be heated and micro-filtered to prolong shelf life, and packers willingly oblige to avoid "product returns" and we might add, to protect their profits.

From Honey Producers. Though difficult to appreciate from a consumer's point of view, there is opposition to a honey standard among honey producers. Here are their reasons:

- Composition of honey varietals varies from region to region and from season to season. Strict standards have the impact of limiting Nature or penalizing the honey producer because of natural occurrences, things for which honey producers should not be held responsible. The fact that honey produced by honeybees from nectar from the Kiawe tree blossoms in Hawaii has more sucrose at certain times of the year than most state standards currently allow presents a reasonable objection to the adoption of a strict standard in that state.

- Making allowances for every potential variation in sucrose content, fructose and glucose ratio, moisture content, or insoluble solid content has the effect of creating too liberal a standard and places too great a burden of proof on the honey producer, especially the smaller ones who may just want to sell their honey at the local farmer's market.

- Contamination of honey by pesticides and herbicides is not always controllable by beekeepers and honey producers. Standards that have mandatory testing requirements for possible contaminants would be onerous for the smaller honey producer and perhaps even for the larger producers who prefer to sell their honey in bulk to packers.

- Some labeling requirements included in existing standards are viewed as unnecessary and impractical. For example, if the standard indicates that honey properly labeled "White Clover Honey" should be found to have less than 45% (or some percentage) of pollen from the white clover flower or a larger percentage of pollen from soybean flowers or alfalfa, the honey producer may be subject to challenge. Some honey producers would argue that they have no control over where the bees fly, but in their best judgment, the honey they produced is "White Clover Honey." Another example is seen in North Carolina where labeling "Sandalwood Honey" as such requires testing and certification from the State, an expense that is paid for by the honey producers.

From Retail (and Wholesale) Outlets. The one party that has the most to lose, at least in the near future, in this discussion of a standard for honey are the stores – grocery, pharmacy, big-box stores – that actually sell honey to consumers. These are the companies with the "deep pockets," and as such have become potential targets for lawsuits brought by consumers who believe that a product they have purchased is or has been misrepresented. It is no coincidence that several lawsuits (at least 12 as of this writing) have been initiated in only those states that have adopted a "Standard of Identity for Honey."

In fact, the retailers might argue that it is specifically because of the standard that they are being sued. Before the standard was adopted in these respective states, they sold the same product without fear or concern of anything other than simple product liability (an accepted risk of doing business typically covered by appropriate liability insurance). Now, they are at risk of having to pay damages for selling a product that may or may not be what the packer or distributor represented it to be. Not a fair turn of events, they argue, especially when the FDA, the federal agency that should be in charge of this sort of thing, has refused to adopt a "Standard of Identity for Honey" in the U.S.

From Regulatory Agencies. There are even reasonable objections to the adoption of a standard for honey from both State and Federal regulatory agencies. Their arguments relate to multiple issues including testing requirements imposed by standards, enforcement issues, interstate commerce issues and economics.

Once a standard is adopted, who is responsible for enforcement? Who pays for testing should such be required by a standard? In an economy like ours, most states are reluctant to add budgetary items for both enforcement and testing to cover a product that represents a very small percentage of overall commodity sales. The hesitancy is amplified for a product for which there is little or no real public health concern regarding its consumption.

Resolving the Tension and Reasons for a Standard for Honey

Given the tension described above and the disparate, disunited nature of the honey industry that exists in the U.S., one might conclude that the whole idea of a Standard of Identity for Honey is just not worth the time and effort required to make it happen. When the first honey standard was adopted in Florida, no one envisioned that it would result in a spate of lawsuits against several reputable retailers and secondarily to include most of the major honey packers in the U.S. That was certainly not the intent. Still, there is reason for the adoption of a honey standard in all states, a standard that serves to benefit all parties–from consumers to honey producers to regulatory agencies.

First and foremost, this is a consumer issue, not a honey industry or packer/importer issue. It is consumers who deserve and should rightfully know what they are purchasing for their family.

Logically, if you buy a product labeled "honey," you should safely assume that honey is what is in the container. If something has been done to the honey in the course of processing it for sale or resale, even if that process has not altered the nature of the honey, you should be so informed. The risk here refers to the unknown. Insufficient research studies have been conducted that compare unprocessed honey straight from the comb to honey that has been heated to 160°F and micro-filtered to remove all pollen and other particular matter. In other words, no one knows for sure if processing makes a difference. What is known can only apply to specific varietals that are used in research.

It is doubtful if anyone (researcher or investigator) will ever attempt to do comprehensive studies to discover if processing, such as the major packers do today, does make a difference in the nature of honey, or in its potential benefits to the consumer. The reasons for that are quite simple. There are over 300 varietals of honey produced in the United States and Canada. Honey is itself, "non-standardized." Medical or scientific studies that have been conducted around the world in the past 20 years have used specific varietals of honey from identifiable sources. Blended honey from multiple sources is never used in research to this writer's knowledge. The economic benefit of studying blended honey is missing, so why consider it?

Honey has been shown in multiple scientific and medical studies to contribute numerous health benefits to consumers. The honey used in these investigative studies is always from a known source or varietal. It can also be assumed that the honey used in these studies contains pollen, has not been micro-filtered, has not been heated, and otherwise meets the criteria used to define and describe honey in the International Codex referred to above. Therefore, when the consumer buys a product labeled "Honey," the realistic expectation should be that what is in the container is honey.

The packer brings to the table another set of issues that would be affected by the adoption of a nationwide standard. Proper labeling for honey when resold should protect the packer from lawsuits. In other words, if the packer does anything to honey in processing (whether to increase shelf life, or to balance constituents to acceptable levels, or to improve color or taste), that product could be sold to the consumer without fear of being sued as long as the packer clearly indicates on the label what process was used, and perhaps for what reason. If the packer heats honey to 160° F, mixes in diatomaceous earth, and micro-filters the honey to remove all particulate matter larger than 5 microns, that product could be sold as "processed" honey or "filtered" honey. The packer in this case may also want to state the reasons why honey is processed in this way as a matter of consumer education. The consumer in this case would be free to make an informed decision as to the nature of the product being purchased.

By the same token, the retailer or reseller of this processed honey would also benefit. They would be free to sell this correctly labeled product along side other "types" of honey. The market would determine which product consumers preferred. Retailers might also benefit in this scenario by marketing the advantages of one honey over another, as in "filtered honey has an extended shelf life" or "buckwheat honey is known for its higher level of antioxidants, a specific benefits to consumers" or "Kiawe honey is pre-crystallized, spreadable, and will remain in this state indefinitely."

The advantages to the honey producer from a honey standard are numerous. First, they would be protected from the unfair competition introduced by the two-tiered market that has emerged in the United States. Cheaper, imported, sometimes adulterated or contaminated, and blended, processed honey typically sells for much less than honey produced by reputable honey producers. While not prohibiting the sale of a cheaper product, a honey standard would level the playing field by introduction of truth-in-labeling. Producers would also be able to take advantage of many marketing advantages linked to the sale and distribution of specific honey varietals. For example, Tupelo honey is known to have an indefinite shelf life (does not crystallize because of its lower glucose and higher fructose content).

Proper labeling as to country of origin would bring advantages to all parties: packers, consumers, retailers, as well as producers. If honey is blended from many sources, including multiple imported sources, the percentage of honey from each country should be clearly stated. The point here is to have the label tell the truth and let the consumer decide their acceptable level of risk when purchasing honey from Vietnam or India or Brazil.

Finally, a honey standard makes sense for everyone. Packers, importers, and honey producers should be free to package and sell products as long as the labels accurately describe those products. For example, "baker's blend" or "industrial honey" is a perfectly legitimate and legal product made up of no more than 49% honey with the rest being a mix of other syrups made from rice or corn. As long as this product is labeled correctly, there should be no prohibition on sales, and the seller should expect protection from unwarranted lawsuits. Consumers should be free to buy cheaper honey products, even sugar-free honey if they choose, as long as they are doing so from an informed basis.

But for now, in the absence of a honey standard in most states, and when in doubt as to the contents of the container labeled "Honey," perhaps it is best to buy honey from a beekeeper whom you know and trust. After all, every beekeeper knows who produces the best honey. Just ask them.

There are important messages for the honey consumer in all of this that must not be overlooked. Honey is a natural product whose identity and purity must be protected, celebrated, and appreciated. In the absence of mandatory standards and regulations, the best recourse for the consumer is to buy honey from local producers whose name and reputation depend on producing a quality product.

Be conscious of price. When you can buy honey in the big box stores at a price less per pound than it takes to produce a pound of honey, it may be wise to question what it is you are buying.

HEALTH BENEFITS OR HEATH CLAIMS–IS THERE A DIFFERENCE?

*"I would feed you with the finest of the wheat, and with **honey** from the rock I would satisfy you." (Psalm 81:16, New Revised Standard Version)*

I t is important to differentiate between a health *benefit* and a health *claim*. The difference is not just semantics, though the terms may seem similar, and are often used interchangeably. Health claims, especially in the United States, are typically validated by controlled, double blind studies conducted within large population or study groups. The results are usually applicable only for that particular study population given the strict protocols by which the research is conducted. Health claims are monitored and reviewed with some degree of scrutiny by the FDA with large fines or other penalties[12] levied for making unsubstantiated and/or unapproved health claims.

Unfortunately, some valid health claims, confirmed by research studies are conveniently ignored or overlooked. There have been numerous observational studies (both animal and human) conducted during the past ten years that link consumption of HFCS to obesity, childhood obesity, and diabetes.[13, 14, 15, 16] The same can be said of sucrose (or table sugar), yet the FDA and most medical organizations remain silent.

Health benefits are no less significant even though they may not have the weight of an FDA-approved health claim. Most readers understand that foods containing antioxidants are good for your health. That is a health benefit statement based on the general knowledge of the role of antioxidants in the body. Foods containing various levels of antioxidants are safely marketed as good for one's health without challenge. A health benefit statement for blueberries, for example, might read, "Contains high levels of antioxidants, which have been found to benefit the nervous system and brain health, and can potentially improve memory." While it is true that no large population studies have been done to date with regard to the health benefits of honey[17], general knowledge of human physiology, as well as information gained from several small research studies (both human and animal), allow us to document and underscore many of the conclusions drawn from these studies over the past couple of decades.

A health benefit is simply something that improves or is of benefit to your general health. No claims are to be inferred as to when, to what degree, or how broadly these benefits apply across a large population. In other words, no statistical calculations are assumed that associate the consumption of honey with reductions in risk of disease. Furthermore, honey is not to be considered a treatment for any disease or condition in a medical or therapeutic sense. All of this does not in any way lesson the fact that honey consumption can be of great benefit to your health. Most importantly, the health benefits derived from consuming honey regularly *come at no risk and with no negative health consequences*, something that cannot be said for any medicine.

Many health benefit statements regarding honey appear throughout this book. These statements are based on facts derived from many sources, including the following:

- Observational studies, using animals or humans
- Small short-term controlled studies, using humans or animals
- Conclusions drawn from "connecting the dots" (linking *accepted knowledge of human physiology* and certain *known or established metabolic principles*.)

When considering the healthful benefits of honey as presented in detail in this book, remember that only pure honey can deliver these benefits. Diluted, adulterated, or imitation products will fall short at best and at worst contribute to the multiple conditions associated with the consumption of sugar, HFCS, other sweeteners, and sugar substitutes.

There is extensive contemporary validation for the many health benefits of honey found in the world's scientific literature, and though some findings are preliminary, results point to the fact that honey possesses extraordinary medicinal properties. *Honey is in a class of its own and can be easily differentiated from other sweeteners when it comes to its metabolism and storage as glycogen in the liver.* Honey's ability to control or eliminate metabolic stress and thereby reduce the risk for many diseases included in the metabolic syndrome[18] borders on miraculous. Honey's role as an effective antimicrobial is just beginning to be appreciated in the western world.

Many of the health benefit statements made in this book will seem outrageous to some or at best counter-intuitive. That is understandable. When first presented with information that regular honey consumption would lower blood sugar levels for most individuals, my own medical training and practice experience protested. Admittedly, it took several months of investigation and repeated review/relearning of basic human physiology to be reassured that indeed this was the case. Observational research studies, some conducted as long ago as 1985 and repeated many times since, have confirmed this fact.[19, 20, 21] More recently, the actual mechanisms detailing how this is possible have been reported.[22] The reader is asked to consider the facts and make informed decisions about personal and family nutritional choices.

HONEY: MORE THAN JUST A SWEETENER

"But Jonathan said, 'My father has troubled the land. Look now, how my countenance has brightened because I tasted a little of this honey.'" (1 Samuel 14:29, New King James Version)

"Conventional wisdom" among many physicians, nutritionists, dietitians, and other health professionals is that honey is only a sugar and needs to be considered as such in relation to any nutritional recommendations for blood sugar control. In fact, the great majority of health professionals hold to this school of thought and practice. Fortunately, conventional wisdom is being overturned by contemporary science and reinforced by anecdotal evidence.

Over the past several months, I have received testimonials from countless individuals who have started consuming honey in an attempt to lower their blood sugar and control their diabetes. One 90 year-old pastor from California tracked his blood sugar levels faithfully every day for one month before starting to consume a tablespoon of honey at bedtime. His daily blood sugar readings averaged 148 milligrams percent (mg%). In the first month after beginning his "honey therapy," his blood sugar levels averaged 138 mg%; the second month, they dropped to an average of 110 mg%, where they remained for an additional six months. His occasional phone calls since that time have assured me that honey continues to keep his diabetes under control.

The mother of a 4 year-old with type 1 diabetes reported that the addition of a one-half teaspoon dose of honey given at bedtime eliminated the wide swings in blood sugar measurements that the child was experiencing.

Others, after beginning a honey regimen, have seen HbA_{1c} levels come down by an average of 0.3 to 0.5% from previous baselines, results that have confounded their physicians. More frequently, fasting blood sugar (FBS) levels (usually taken the first thing in the morning or upon awakening) were reported as being lower by 10 to 20 mg%, especially when honey was consumed just before bedtime. When offering the explanation that consuming honey was the reason blood sugar levels have stabilized, FBS levels were lower and their HbA_{1c} levels have come down, the disbelieving physician often responded by saying, "That can't be so. Honey is only a sugar!"

The physician is, of course, speaking the truth. Honey is composed of two principle sugars, glucose and fructose, just the same as HFCS and sucrose. The ratio of fructose to glucose in all three sweeteners is nearly the same (one to one, or close to it). The difference between these sugars, how they are metabolized, and exactly how they work in the human system is the part that seems to be misunderstood by many physicians.

The most intriguing aspect of this positive effect of honey consumption on blood sugar measurements is that it seems to work better and more consistently in older folks and/or in individuals who have more advanced glucose intolerance due to developing or pre-existing insulin resistance.[23] That should be extremely good news for those caught in the advancing cycle of age and increased dependence on medication(s) to control blood sugar.

Tom's Story
[Adapted from *Feed Your Brain First*]

A t age 22, Tom was a picture of fitness and health: 74 inches tall, 180 pounds, sculpted abs and upper torso, powerful legs and muscular arms. He had completed college, where he was a star running back on the football team. He married and in time entered the workforce as an investment broker, where he was chained to a desk with a computer terminal for hours each day for weeks on end that extended into years and then into decades. During his 20s and 30s, he had continued running, putting in 20 to 30 miles a week on the track or treadmill. He had even completed a handful of marathons.

Time Changes Things

Now at age 55, time and lifestyle had taken a toll. Tom weighed in at 270 pounds; his body still was sculpted but in a more "settled" and rounded way. His health was measured by numbers, not number of miles run per week, but numbers like 260 (cholesterol) and 7.6 (HbA_{1c}) and 150/96 (blood pressure).

In addition to the obvious changes in Tom's appearance, something more sinister was taking place within Tom's body, something that Tom could not appreciate.

Sleep patterns were changing and his wife complained about an increase in snoring. Tolerance for mild to moderate exercise was decreasing. Midday fatigue and excessive sleepiness were beginning to affect work. He was always hungry, or so it seemed, consuming snacks and soft drinks throughout the day. Mornings were miserable as he awakened feeling shaky, fatigued and often nauseous, able only to gulp down a cup of coffee before heading out the door to work.

Tom's story is a classic illustration of life in the 21st century for thousands, even millions of folks. Tom's doctor diagnosed type 2 diabetes, hyperlipidemia (elevated cholesterol and triglycerides) and hypertension (high blood pressure), politely leaving out obesity, and prescribed several pills to treat his "diseases" and control his numbers. (This approach characterizes much of modern medicine. "Treat the numbers" rather than the cause.)

An Inside Look

To unravel the genesis of Tom's progressively deteriorating health, role back the clock and take another picture of Tom – a word picture that looks at what's taking place on the inside rather than the outside. This is a picture that you won't find described in any medical chart or textbook, yet nevertheless, one that is just as important, perhaps more important than if Tom's doctor had written it.

The picture that you are about to have revealed focuses on one organ – the liver – and its role in providing fuel for the brain. Admittedly, the liver is not a very sexy organ. It is seldom publically portrayed in any disease scenario except the conditions caused by alcohol, infectious agents or cancer. No one inquires about the liver in casual conversations like they might about the heart or stomach or other more visible body parts. *Yet the liver is at the heart of Tom's progressively poor health.*

The reason? Tom was genetically predisposed to be a 180-pound male. His body parts, including his internal organs, were perfectly proportioned to support and sustain a man at that weight. At maturity, his *liver* weighed approximately 1.6 kg (3.5 pounds) and could manufacture and store about 80 to 90 grams of glycogen at any given time, enough to sustain his brain, kidneys and red blood cells through eight hours or so of sleep or one hour of intense physical exercise. At age 55, Tom's metabolic demands were increased by at least one-third over those at age 22, perhaps by as much as 50%. His resting heart rate was faster. His blood pressure was up because his heart had to pump blood through more than 9,000 miles of additional blood vessels to circulate blood through the additional 90 pounds of fat.

Keeping Up with Demand Only Makes Things Worse

Part of the energy for this increased demand could be made up for by increased consumption. For several years, Tom tried to keep pace, but the more he consumed, the more demand he placed on his metabolic requirements and the more glucose intolerant he became. Furthermore, the more carbohydrates Tom consumed, the greater was his demand for insulin production, and the less effective his insulin became in partitioning glucose into the cells. His body was becoming "insulin resistant."

In addition, Tom's fat stores were themselves colossal consumers of glucose, requiring increased amounts of energy just to maintain the hugely increased storage capacity. Tom's liver glycogen store was being depleted at an excessive rate, just to maintain peripheral fat deposits.

The Starving Brain Is a Greedy Brain

Tom's brain fuel reserve tank, rather than having enough glycogen on board for eight hours of sleep, was running on low within four hours of retiring to bed. Compounded by poor eating habits, and the failure to restock his liver before bedtime with glycogen, Tom was experiencing *chronic brain starvation* night after night. Another way to say this is that Tom's brain was "out of gas." Tom's brain reacted to this energy deficit by initiating a protective mechanism called *metabolic stress*. That means that his brain triggered the release of the adrenal hormones (adrenalin and cortisol) to ensure that adequate fuel for the brain was being created during a time when no food was being ingested. Metabolic stress awakened Tom early in the morning and resulted in poor quality and interrupted sleep or *chronic sleep loss*. (It should be clear to all that adrenalin is not a sleeping aid.)

Excessive cortisol released night after night, as in Tom's case, had a serious negative impact on his glucose metabolism rendering the insulin that his body did produce less effective over time. Eventually, this resulted in glucose intolerance, insulin resistance and type 2 diabetes.

Tom's excessive consumption of calories over the years, mostly from carbohydrates, had resulted in a condition we call *chronic brain starvation*. This resulted in even more demands for energy, more consumption of food, more metabolic stress, poor quality sleep, and increased risk for the dreaded diseases of aging including memory impairments and Alzheimer's disease. Tom had entered the downward spiral of life experienced prematurely by so many in midlife.

When the Liver Is the "Heart" of the Problem

Earlier, we said that the liver was at the heart of Tom's problem. Let's connect a few more dots. As Tom reached physical maturity, his liver size and capacity to store glycogen topped out at about 80 to 90 grams. At age 55, his liver glycogen storage capacity was still only 80 to 90 grams, possibly a bit less as dietary abuses over the years, such as the excessive consumption of HFCS, would have contributed to a fatty liver.[24] Alcohol use may have also decreased the ability of his liver to process and store glucose.[25]

During the midlife years and later, Tom's need for liver glycogen was increased above the norm. Instead of ten grams per hour at rest, Tom's body demanded significantly more glycogen per hour to sustain his brain, red blood cells and kidneys, and also the increasing peripheral mass of tissue he had accumulated over the years.

When Tom retired for bed after the late evening TV news, his liver glycogen store was already partially depleted. His last meal consumed about 6:00 PM may have added some to the glycogen store, but by bedtime, Tom may have had only 30 to 40 grams of liver glycogen remaining, enough for only three to four hours of brain fuel during sleep. By 2:30 AM his liver was signaling his brain that a fuel crisis was nearing. His brain reacted in the normal way to secure a new food supply by waking Tom up with an adrenalin and cortisol release, designed to produce new glucose from his body's protein, thus contributing to his chronic sleep loss.

Starving in the Land of Plenty

Tom's system was flush with fuel all the time. He ate excessively and frequently. His blood sugar levels were consistently high, compatible with his food intake. His fat stores were abundant and constantly being renewed and replenished. He lived with an abundance of stored energy. *The sad irony was that Tom's brain was increasingly and repeatedly being starved.* Medication for his diabetes, hyperlipidemia and hypertension did nothing to correct his underlying problem. His treatment was directed at reducing his "numbers" rather than correcting the cause.

His brain was constantly competing for fuel with his increasing body mass and the result was *repeated nighttime metabolic stress.* His liver was unable to create and store glycogen because of metabolic stress and therefore unable to stock sufficient fuel reserve for the brain.

Every Man's (and Every Woman's) Story
"Tom's story is a medical metaphor for what is experienced by millions of Americans."

Tom's story is not unique. The specific numbers and the progression of the pathology may vary somewhat from person to person, male to female, but generally, Tom is a medical metaphor for millions of Americans diagnosed with adult onset diabetes (type 2 diabetes), insulin resistance, obesity, hypertension, hyperlipidemia, cardiovascular disease, osteoporosis, and even Alzheimer's disease.

Not everyone will share Tom's experience. There are many factors that influence the manifestation of disease and the intensity or severity of symptoms. Certainly genetics plays an important role, as does diet, lifestyle, environmental exposure and many other factors. Yet the truth is that many of the diseases and conditions afflicting individuals living in the 21st century are variations of those experienced by Tom. They all have their origins in what physicians have referred to since the 1990s as *the metabolic syndrome.*

At the center of all of these diseases and conditions are the three common threads mentioned above: *chronic brain starvation, chronic sleep loss* and *chronic metabolic stress.*[26] The way these threads intertwine and manifest themselves in people may vary across a wide range of outcomes, yet all share the same causal elements. Not everyone who is overweight gets diabetes. Not everyone who is skinny has normal blood glucose metabolism. Some develop osteoporosis. Some have thyroid deficiency. Others are depressed. Many are destined to have an early onset of Alzheimer's disease or Parkinsonism or other forms of neuro-degenerative diseases. Some get cancer or coronary artery disease. Many have hypertension or become handicapped from strokes. Others just sleep poorly every night.

The interventions and therapies that are offered by contemporary medicine to combat these diseases and conditions are multiple and varied, and to state the obvious, expensive! Wouldn't it be better to just prevent these conditions from occurring in the first place? You may think that to be a preposterous idea. Just give me a pill! Pills treat the numbers and do little to change underlying causes of disease. All of the diseases and conditions experienced by Tom may be simply prevented. In many cases, the progression of symptoms can be easily arrested or reversed.

IS YOUR DIETARY SHIFT SHOWING?

"If you obey, you will enjoy a long life in the land the LORD swore to give to your ancestors and to you, their descendants — a land flowing with milk and honey!" (Deuteronomy 11: 9, New Living Translation)

The significance of honey in nutritional considerations might be lost completely if it were not for a not-so-subtle event that has been occurring over the past 50 years in the United States — an event characterized by the shift away from fats in our diet to a predominance of carbohydrates. This dietary shift has produced results that we can all see firsthand, whether in our daily glances in the mirror or while "people gazing." These results should not surprise anyone. Any cattle farmer knows how to fatten cattle for market — just feed them corn for a few months, which is nearly 80% glucose. An understanding of this shift and how it has occurred argues for increased consumption of honey and underscores why the differences between honey and other sweeteners as detailed in the next chapter are important.

Since the 1970s, when new conventional wisdom began to emphasize an avoidance of saturated fats and

the fat-free food craze got its start, a tragic result of epidemic proportions has occurred. The marketing success
of this national fat avoidance message could be touted
as a major achievement of the processed food industry
if it were not for its adverse consequences. Fat-free (high
carbohydrate) foods are marketed as "heart healthy."
Low-fat or fat-free foods that replace relatively harmless
amounts of fats from natural foods with excess sugar
and HFCS have flooded the market, supposedly offering
a healthier option. You can even find vegetables sold as
"fat-free" in the frozen food section (foods that never
contained an ounce of fat in the first place). And gullible
folks, believing that they are choosing a healthy option
for themselves and their families have responded. The
direct result of this dietary shift is that two out of three
individuals in the United States is overweight or obese,
which includes 20% of children under the age of 18.

Over 24 million U.S. citizens have diabetes (nearly
10% of the population) and a staggering 57 million are
pre-diabetic. The economic costs are enormous, now
exceeding $245 billion annually for diabetes alone.[27]

Of course there are causes for this epidemic shift
other than just the increased consumption of carbohydrates. Sedentary lifestyles, lack of exercise, increased
dependence on technology, reduction in physical labor,
genetics, and even economics — all can be blamed. But
the preponderance of evidence relating to our weighty
health problem corresponds, not so coincidently, to this
marked shift in the percentage of carbohydrates being
consumed in our diets each day, especially from refined
cane and beet sugars and HFCS.[28]

A major irony in this dietary shift is that while fat is
epidemic, fats are not the problem! What started in the
1960s as the "dietary fat hypothesis" has resulted in the
largest public health issue of this new century. In the late

1940s, the Framingham Heart Study in Massachusetts began collecting data on 8,000 men. By the mid 1960s, it appeared that saturated fats in the diet were apparently associated with an increased incidence of cardiovascular disease (heart attacks, strokes, and high blood pressure). From this apparent association came the widely accepted mantra "beware of saturated fats," and over the next two decades, fat-free or low-fat *everything or anything* became the accepted norm.

It was not until 1992 that Dr. William Castelli, the original director of the Framingham Study, blew the whistle on this myth that had by that time become an accepted fact by nearly everyone. In an article published in the *Archives of Internal Medicine,* Dr. Castelli stated, *"the people with the lowest serum cholesterol* were the ones who *ate the most saturated fat and cholesterol,* and took in the most calories"[29] (emphasis added). In other words, the amount of dietary fats should not necessarily be associated with elevated fat (cholesterol and triglyceride) measurements from your blood or serum. Such indictment of dietary fats continues, in spite of the lack of scientific evidence to support it.

Another irony in this dietary shift is that fat-free foods (especially processed foods) are actually more problematic, contributing to the fat epidemic rather than reducing it. One critical observation is that it didn't take long for processed food manufacturers to discover just how to make fat-free or low-fat foods taste good: just add sugar or HFCS. So much sugar and HFCS has been added and consumed during the age of processed foods that the *annual per capita* consumption of these sweeteners now exceeds 125 pounds — nearly 2 ½ pounds per week.

The unheralded truth about human metabolism is that you do not get fat by eating fat.[30] *You get fat by eating too much sugar!* Beware of products marketed as fat-free or low-fat or heart healthy on the packaging. Check the label for sugar or HFCS content and decide for yourself if it is worth the risk.

One product in particular that illustrates this marketing sleight of hand is fat-free, low-fat or light yogurt. Food manufacturers have flooded the market with these products, which now occupy several shelves of the supermarket coolers. The irony is that relatively small amounts of harmless milk fats are removed and excessive quantities of sugar or HFCS or both are added. Then, supported by huge advertising budgets, these products are promoted as a healthy option. *The reality is that regular yogurt sweetened with a small amount of honey is much better for you.*

The World Health Organization (WHO) and other public health advisory groups recommend that no more than 40% of your daily caloric intake should come from carbohydrates. No more than 10% of your total calorie intake each day should come from simple sugars (sucrose, glucose, or HFCS) that have been added to foods. As of March 2014, WHO reduced this recommendation to no more than 5% of total calories from simple sugars, but in so doing, included honey and other syrups in the total amount of simple sugars allowed, indicating that WHO believes that honey is no different than other sugars. This, as we shall see later in this book is an unfortunate oversight at best. Today, 60 to 80% (and sometimes more) of our current daily caloric intake comes from carbohydrates — nearly double the recommended amount. More than half comes directly from simple sugars or HFCS added to foods or beverages rather than from naturally occurring sugars as in honey, fruits, and vegetables.[31]

The 40-year period from the late 1950s though the 1990s experienced a progressive rise in the amount of refined sugar and HFCS consumed (especially after 1971 when HFCS was first produced), leading to a peak consumption in 1999. Today the consumption of sweeteners has leveled out somewhat.[32] A conservative estimate of the *total daily per capita consumption of sweeteners is 161 grams (0.35 pounds), or 644 calories.* One estimate suggests that the top 20% of high caloric sweetener users ingests *a whopping 3160 calories from HFCS alone per day.*[33] Compare that to the recommendation made by the American Heart Association in March of 2010.[34] Their benchmark was 25 grams (100 calories) per day for women and 37.5 grams (150 calories) for men. That amount doesn't include the natural sugars that are found in fruits, vegetables, and milk products.

Though the cause and effect relationship between excessive sugar consumption and obesity is being debated in the scientific literature, common sense would indicate a connection. Is there any wonder why we are a generation of fat people?

Simple Carbohydrate Consumption:
Actual versus Recommended

Actual Carbohydrate Consumption from Sweeteners

161 grams (0.35 pounds) per day = Average Consumption

Versus Recommended Amount

37.5 grams/day = Maximum amount recommended for adult males (150 calories)

25 grams/day = Maximum amount recommended for adult females (100 calories)

EXCESS amount of Sweeteners consumed per day = 123.5 to 136 grams or 1/4 to nearly 1/3 pound for every man, woman, and child

---

Nutrition Labels Can Be Deceiving

When you look on the nutrition facts for any food product requiring such a label, starch (glucose) is sometimes not listed but included as part of the total carbohydrates. Sometimes starch is listed separately from sugars, wrongly implying that starch is something other than sugar (glucose).

If you look at the nutrition facts for one large potato weighing about 300 grams, you will see that it contains 63 grams of carbohydrates and 4 grams of sugar. Wouldn't you infer from this information that the remaining 59 grams of carbohydrate in this potato were made up of something other than sugar? The truth is those 59 grams are composed of fiber (7 grams) and starch (52 grams), both of which are *sugars*, mostly glucose.

Another good example is corn. The nutrition label will tell you a cup of corn provides 31 grams of carbohydrate, and *only five grams of sugar*. The remainder of the carbohydrates is listed as 21.4 grams of starch, which is *nothing but glucose, a simple sugar*. Whether intentional or not, this labeling is quite deceptive to the food shopper who actually reads labels.

The majority of us in the medical and scientific communities are uninformed, driven by pharmaceutical "solutions" and pressured by a results oriented "can't you just give me a pill, Doc?" society. The rest of us who depend on the experts to keep us healthy and provide us with up-to-date information are confused as we learn that **nutritional advice that we believed to be true in our generation has produced more obesity, diabetes, and neuro-degenerative diseases than during any other time in the history of our nation**.

What we do know is taking a very long time to make its way into practical conventional wisdom useful for today's population. There are many reasons for this.

Oversight, ignorance, and marketing money from the processed foods industry are having a disastrous effect on our public health in epidemic proportions. Even our federal agencies that have all the data and should know better are complicit in not providing the correct information. Professional organizations and associations that are controlled or strongly influenced by special interests and their huge marketing budgets, focus on costly interventions well after the damage has been done, rather than on prevention.

Practice versus Prevention and the Control of Blood Sugar

Medical practice, generally speaking, prefers intervention and treatment over prevention. Yet for all the good it does, medicine is losing the war on obesity, diabetes, and the many other diseases and conditions directly caused by or associated with faulty or impaired glucose metabolism. The solutions are relatively simple. However, an almost universal blindness has succeeded in keeping what should have been apparent, out of the mainstream of public health and medical practice.

In no area of medical practice is this dichotomy – the contrasting approach between *treatment* and *prevention* of the underlying cause of a condition – more focused than in the consideration of blood sugar or blood glucose. Over the past half century, blood sugar measurement has evolved into the *sine qua non* of human metabolism evaluation. Patients are informed that they are pre-diabetic or diabetic based on the value of this measurement and other associated lab values such as HbA_{1c}.[35] Drug companies have made fortunes formulating medicines that can reduce the numbers and regulate blood sugar within a "normal range."[36]

Blood sugar, except in both extremes of excessively high and low measurements, is quite an irrelevant number. It is transient, rapidly changing, and subject to strict regulation within the body. *Blood sugar measurement does not give us a reliable indication of fuel availability for the brain, except in the very short term (a few minutes at best), just as water flowing from the tap is not a measure of water availability, except in the short term.* In other words, the blood sugar measurement may be within a normal range while at the same instant, the brain's fuel supply is depleted placing the brain in imminent danger. The same may also be true when the blood glucose is elevated on a chronic basis. Such conditions exist for a large majority of folks every day and night for weeks at a time, without their knowledge and irrespective of blood sugar levels. The result is a metabolic condition that we have referred to above as metabolic stress.

Understanding Carbohydrates and Carbohydrate Metabolism

Quite simply, carbohydrates are foods that are made up mostly of starch or sugar. We think of them primarily as plant based (come from plants) with the one big exception being lactose, a sugar found in milk. Scientists think of carbohydrates synonymously with saccharides (or sugars) that exist either as single molecules (monosaccharides such as glucose or fructose) or two or more molecules joined together (disaccharides such as sucrose or lactose, or oligosaccharides and polysaccharides such as starch or glycogen).

Underscore this fact: *carbohydrates are sugars*. And don't get confused by the "good carbs, bad carbs" debate. *Carbs are sugar. It's just that simple.*

Most of us know the foods that are high in carbohydrates. The list includes bread, potatoes, rice, whole grains, vegetables, pastas, cereals and most anything made from flour, or corn and other grains. Carbohydrates are the most common source of energy for living organisms, and glucose is the *king of carbohydrates*. Carbohydrates are all high in starch.[37] *Starch is glucose!*

However, *carbohydrates are not essential in the human diet*. The fact that glucose is the *king of carbohydrates* stands in direct contradiction to the fact that *carbohydrates are not essential nutrients in humans*. The body can obtain all its energy requirements from proteins and fats. These statements are almost counter-intuitive to our overindulgent carbohydrate-saturated society, but the fact remains, the body can make all the glucose it requires for fuel out of proteins or amino acids.

From the perspective of the brain, it may appear to be a significant irony to label carbohydrates as *non-essential*. After all, the brain and its individual cells (neurons) rely almost entirely on glucose for energy. It cannot burn fat except under limited and harsh conditions. The brain will use certain amino acids from proteins for fuel, but only in small amounts and only when they are available.

The facts about sugars and carbohydrates can be summarized as follows:

1. All carbohydrates are sugars. All starches are carbohydrates. Therefore, all starches are sugars.
2. Carbohydrates are **nonessential** for human metabolism and energy needs.
3. Glucose is a carbohydrate, a simple sugar. Glucose is **essential** for brain fuel, the exclusive fuel selected by the brain for its energy needs.
4. Glucose can be manufactured within the body from amino acids and thus is **nonessential** (from dietary sources).

5. The brain's requirement for glucose takes priority over all other metabolic considerations in the body.
6. When excessive amounts of simple sugars such as glucose and fructose are ingested by themselves from starchy foods or in beverages and processed foods to which HFCS or sucrose have been added, the body stores them as fat.
7. The *average* American consumes *four to six times the amount of simple sugars daily than recommended* for good health.
8. Honey is made up primarily of carbohydrates, but as we shall see in the next chapter, *honey contains other substances that allow it to be metabolized, stored, and utilized in the body quite differently than other carbohydrates.*

DIFFERENTIATING HONEY FROM OTHER SWEETENERS

*"I'll take you to a land sweeter by far than this one, a land of grain and wine, bread and vineyards, olive orchards and **honey**. You only live once–so live, really live!" (2 Kings 18:32, The Message)*

What makes honey unique? Or more simply put, "Why honey?" On what basis can you distinguish honey from its competitors? Given the fact that honey contains the same sugars as HFCS and table sugar – glucose and fructose, in nearly the same ratio – what makes honey so different? To better appreciate the role of honey as a healthful food, it is first helpful to look at the sweeteners to which honey is frequently compared.

Sucrose. Sucrose, or common table sugar, is a simple sugar — a disaccharide made up of equal parts of two sugars, glucose and fructose. When ingested, an enzyme in the gut breaks the bond holding the fructose and glucose molecules together, allowing them to pass easily into the blood stream. The circulating blood then delivers the fructose and glucose to the liver and on to other cells of the body. The liver immediately converts both fructose and glucose into glycogen for storage within the liver cells *until the storage capacity is met* (usually about 75 grams). Some of the excess amounts of both sugars (especially fructose) is converted into fats and stored in the liver cells.

Glucose not converted to glycogen in the liver remains in the circulation causing blood sugar levels to rise resulting in the release of excessive amounts of insulin from the pancreas. Excessive consumption of sucrose is associated with obesity, diabetes, insulin resistance, and the metabolic syndrome and its associated conditions.[38] It has been said that if FDA approval of sugar as a food additive were to be requested today, it would be denied! [39]

Glucose. Glucose in your diet comes from many sources, the most common being foods to which sucrose and HFCS have been added. Additional glucose comes from fruits and vegetables, especially starchy foods like rice, potatoes, pasta, corn and grains from which flour is made.

Glucose can be used for energy by nearly every cell in the body. When more glucose is consumed at any one time than can be converted to glycogen and stored in the liver, the excess amount remains in the circulating blood as blood sugar. Facilitated by the action of insulin, glucose in the blood enters the body's cells where it is used for energy, stored as glycogen in muscle cells for later use, or converted to fat for storage in adipose (fatty) tissue around the abdominal organs. The amount of glucose that is converted to fat is directly related to the intensity of your activity level, and the storage capacity of both the liver and the muscle cells.

Fructose. Fructose, like glucose, is a simple sugar, a monosaccharide. It is found primarily in fruit and since the 1970s, in processed foods and beverages containing

HFCS. Both fructose and glucose when consumed in excess and combined with protein can be a significant cause of cellular damage in diabetics, thus contributing to many age-related chronic inflammatory diseases.[40, 41] While glucose can be used by every cell in the body for energy, *fructose can only be metabolized in the liver*. And unlike glucose, lower insulin levels and less appetite hormones are produced as a result of fructose consumption.

Consumption of excessive amounts of fructose is associated with a likelihood of obesity[42] and elevated levels of triglycerides.[43] Dr. Meira Field, a research chemist at the USDA made this statement about fructose, "the liver of rats on the high fructose diet looked like the livers of alcoholics, plugged with fat and cirrhotic," an observation confirmed by research published in 2008.[44]

High Fructose Corn Syrup (HFCS). HFCS is made from cornstarch, which is mostly glucose. Enzymatic action catalyzed by hydrochloric acid produces fructose from the glucose. Once the solution reaches a concentration of 90% fructose, glucose is added to arrive at the ratios commonly used in food manufacturing and processing today, either a 55:45 or 42:58 ratio of fructose to glucose. HFCS is technically not *high fructose*, but a balanced ratio close to the 1:1 ratio found in sucrose or honey.

HFCS represents about 40% of the sweeteners used in foods and beverages in the United States. Until recently, 100% of the soft drinks bottled in the U.S. used HFCS as the primary sweetener. Now, the negative publicity surrounding HFCS has forced bottling companies to begin using sugar again. The same is also occurring in food processing, with food manufacturers boldly proclaiming, "Contains no HFCS," on their package labels.

What is not being told, however, is that *HFCS and sugar (sucrose) consumption have just the same effects in the body.*[45]

What is the problem with sugar and HFCS? Don't they have similar fructose to glucose ratios and the same caloric density as honey? That's the argument used by the Corn Refiners Association on their website. The challenge for the honey industry and for those who drive public health policy is to *differentiate* honey from other sweeteners. As the demand for and consumption of other sweeteners declines commensurate with an increase in information as to the disastrous health effects of these sweeteners, the consumption of honey will also decrease unless the consumer is educated and informed.

What makes honey different? On the surface, this is a formidable challenge. When comparing honey, table sugar (sucrose), and HFCS strictly on the fructose and glucose content alone, there is little difference between them. However, beyond the initial similarities, honey is a unique natural food that can be differentiated from sugar and HFCS by several distinct physiologic events that occur within the body when it is ingested. These events are due to several mechanisms of action (reasons why honey acts as it does) and can be grouped into three overlapping categories as follows:

- The natural constituents contained in each product,
- The prebiotic effects of each product, and
- The metabolic results that occur after consumption of each.

The Natural Constituents. Honey contains more than 180 different substances that have been isolated from various honey varietals. These include 5 enzymes,

6 different vitamins, 8 distinctive lipids, 12 minerals, 17 trace elements, 18 different acids, 18 amino acids (proteins), 18 bioflavonoids (also known as antioxidants), and 26 aroma compounds. In this regard, *honey is more like a fruit than a sugar*. Sucrose, from either cane or beets, and HFCS are much simpler compounds by comparison, made up primarily of the simple sugars, glucose and fructose.

Within the past few years, substances in honey have been identified that help to regulate the production of a protein hormone produced in the liver, known as hepatic insulin sensitizing substance (HISS). HISS release from the liver facilitates the uptake of glucose into muscle cells where it is stored as glycogen, thus resulting in lower blood sugar levels. In other words, substances found in honey contribute to lowering of blood sugar levels unlike sucrose, glucose (starch), or HFCS, which immediately raise blood sugar.

Several of the natural constituents of honey act as powerful antioxidants within the body. Others work to lower inflammation within the cells and tissues. Neither the antioxidant nor anti-inflammatory properties of honey are found in sucrose or HFCS. In fact, these sugars produce significant inflammatory effects, both within the gut and within cells throughout the body.

The Prebiotic Effects. Other natural constituents of honey are complex sugars known as oligosaccharides that some researchers also believe contribute to the anti-diabetic effect of honey as well as produce beneficial effects on lipid (fat) levels.[51] These oligosaccharides are not digested in the upper gastrointestinal tract as the simple sugars found in honey, but make their way into the large intestine where they serve as prebiotics[52] for microorganisms found in the gut.

It is this finding that seems to be related to the positive effect of consuming honey on conditions such as obesity, insulin resistance and diabetes as well as reduction of lipids (triglycerides and cholesterol). Simple sugars such as sucrose, glucose, and HFCS contain no complex sugars and have no similar prebiotic effects.

The Metabolic Results after Consumption. Honey is metabolized, stored, and utilized in the body differently than sucrose, glucose or HFCS. The reasons for this are not only related to the additional natural constituents found in honey as well as the prebiotic effects, but also to the marked differences in glucose uptake into the cells when blood sugar levels are elevated, a condition that exists frequently and repeatedly when excessive amounts of sucrose, glucose or HFCS are consumed.

The body has two primary storage areas for glucose: muscle tissue and the liver. When these storage reserves are full, the excess glucose is converted to and stored as fat. Because of the natural constituents found in honey that regulate insulin release as well as the prebiotic effects that limit fat formation, a small dose of honey (1 to 2 tablespoons, or 20 to 40 grams), with its nearly equal glucose and fructose ratio, results in a lower blood sugar level, less fat storage, and optimum replenishment of liver glycogen levels. *Honey ingestion results in the most rapid and efficient formation of liver glycogen of any natural food.*

Sucrose and HFCS in the amounts typically ingested in the average daily diet result in quite different outcomes. *The excessive ingestion of glucose,[47] sucrose, and HFCS in the modern diet results in elevated blood sugar levels and increased fat storage, a result not found when honey is consumed in moderation.*

In addition, the typical load of fructose (contained in sucrose or HFCS[48]) consumed by the average person is simply overwhelming to the liver, which is the only organ that can metabolize fructose. The liver stops everything else that it is doing, including the production of glycogen, to metabolize fructose. It does this by converting the fructose into trioses, or three-carbon molecules, which enter the fatty acid cycle to form triglycerides. Triglycerides produced in excess are stored as fat. In other words, glycogen (brain fuel) formation is halted in order for the liver to deal with the excessive amount of fructose coming down the metabolic conveyor belt. *Excessive fructose ingestion results in fat formation and storage – a problem that does not occur when small amounts of fructose (as found in honey or fruit) are consumed.*

A Honey Tolerance Test (similar to the Glucose Tolerance Test, or GTT) is another confirmation[49] of how honey results in lower blood sugar levels than those produced when other sugars are ingested. A dose of honey is ingested and blood sugar levels are measured at several intervals following administration; the same is done with glucose or sucrose at a separate time. When compared to the glucose and sucrose tests, results from the honey tests at 60 and 90 minutes after consumption show a 20 and 40 mg% lower blood sugar level respectively.[50]

Together, these compositional, prebiotic, and metabolic effects of consuming natural unprocessed honey differentiate honey from table sugar, glucose and HFCS.

All Sugars Are Not the Same

It is at this point in the narrative that someone usually asks, "Despite all its good qualities, wouldn't consuming the same amount of honey as sucrose or HFCS produce the same harmful effects as other sugar excesses do?" The answer lies in the book of Wisdom in the Old Testament:

"If you find honey, eat just enough — too much of it, and you will vomit." (Proverbs 25:16, New International Version)

It is safe to conclude, without personal experimentation, that this is a true statement: the body does not tolerate well the ingestion of excessive levels of honey (quite unlike that which occurs following consumption of excess levels of sugar or HFCS which are absorbed and processed without any immediate side effects).

The following list summarizes the most important events that occur within the body when honey is consumed on a regular basis. Later in the book, these general events or mechanisms of action will be correlated with specific diseases and conditions for which honey might be helpful, along with updated research references supporting these facts. Other references can be found in earlier books in *The Honey Revolution* series.

1. *Honey produces more liver glycogen than any other food on a gram-for-gram basis. It is the gold standard of carbohydrates for producing and storing liver glycogen*, the primary fuel reserve for the brain.

2. *Honey stabilizes (regulates and controls) blood sugar levels.* In other words, *honey lowers blood sugar, as well as prevents low blood sugar.* Glucose from honey enters the liver directly to form liver glycogen. As the sugars in honey are removed from the blood and stored in the liver as glycogen, hyperglycemia (high blood sugar) is reduced and blood sugar levels are maintained within a normal range. Hyperglycemia over time leads to the development of insulin resistance, which is the primary cause of intracellular oxidative stress. Honey, stored as liver glycogen, is

released on demand during sleep and exercise, thus preventing episodes of hypoglycemia (low blood sugar).

3. *Honey consumption results in a lower insulin response than that produced by the ingestion of similar amounts of sucrose or HFCS, thus delaying or preventing the development of insulin resistance.* Insulin resistance and intracellular oxidative stress are the underlying causes of many diseases and conditions associated with the metabolic syndrome and diseases of aging.

4. *Honey consumption reduces intracellular inflammation* associated with diabetes and aging.

5. *Honey consumption has a direct effect on lowering cortisol levels* throughout the body by its promotion of liver glycogen formation, regulation of blood sugar, and prevention of metabolic stress. Metabolic stress occurs when the brain's fuel supply is low, as during exercise or sleep. Honey consumption can help to ensure an adequate store of liver glycogen for the brain, thus preventing or reducing the release of stress hormones (adrenalin and cortisol) from the adrenal glands.

6. *Honey consumption reduces metabolic stress thus reducing the risks for many of the diseases and conditions associated with the metabolic syndrome,* including obesity, diabetes, and cardiovascular disease.

7. *Daily honey consumption will lower triglyceride and cholesterol levels and increase HDL (good) cholesterol.* The fructose in honey actually protects against triglyceride formation.

8. *Honey consumption before bedtime promotes restorative sleep and improves sleep quality and duration.*

Restorative sleep reduces risk for hypertension and other metabolic conditions and diseases.

9. *Honey lowers levels of homocysteine* (HCY), a metabolite of the amino acid methionine involved in cellular metabolism and the manufacture of proteins. Elevated HCY levels are responsible for about 10% of the coronary deaths each year in the United States.

10. *Honey consumption improves memory and cognitive ability* by reducing the amount of cortisol released during metabolic stress.

11. *Honey improves immune system functioning*, thus improving allergy symptoms.

12. *Honey consumption indirectly lowers overall cancer risks* and improves the body's ability to fight cancer by several known mechanisms of action, including impeding the replication and growth of cancer cells and improving immune system functioning.

13. *The fructose from honey facilitates the detoxification of alcohol* by restoring NAD, the liver enzyme responsible for metabolizing alcohol.

These health benefits and more can be experienced by the simple strategy of consuming honey daily. There is no risk and the positive health consequences might be life changing.

It Is Counterintuitive but True

Of the 13 health benefits listed above, the effect of honey consumption on blood sugar is restated for emphasis. This fact seems so counterintuitive (sort of like eating bacon to lower your cholesterol) as to be discounted by most physicians and nutritionists. The keys to honey's ability to regulate blood sugar are its balance

of fructose and glucose, the additional natural constituents not found in sugar or HFCS, and the effect on blood
sugar levels compared to other sugars. As fructose in
honey facilitates the incorporation of glucose into the
liver to form glycogen, glucose is removed from circulation and blood sugar levels are lowered. Fructose itself
is also converted to glycogen in the liver by a simple
enzymatic process that occurs only in liver cells.

Honey consumption resulting in the direct formation of liver glycogen serves several purposes. A full
liver glycogen store provides the body with immediate
access to glucose at any time when blood sugar levels
are low, such as during exercise or while sleeping, or in
situations known as reactive hypoglycemia. The liver
glycogen store fuels the brain, kidneys and red blood
cells (tissues which do not have a fuel reserve of their
own) around the clock and at times when these tissues
are most at risk of running out of fuel, such as during
exercise and during the nighttime, when no food is
being ingested. At all times, the liver releases its glycogen store on demand to share with all other organs
in the body. *Honey is the gold standard of foods that form
liver glycogen.*[53]

Becky's Story
(Adapted from *The Honey Revolution – Abridged*)

B ecky had a successful career as an administrative assistant for a corporate VP for more than thirty years. Her life was packed with episodic stress on the job that began most mornings at 6:00 AM and lasted into the evening hours, five to six days a week.

Her eating patterns were as consistent as work demands allowed, yet frequently she suffered from bouts of shakiness, lightheadedness, nausea, and diminished concentration. Her sleep was punctuated with bouts of wakefulness and she awakened most mornings at 4:30 AM not feeling rested. Wake-ups were especially difficult and symptomatic.

Her self-diagnosis was "low blood sugar" and her solution was to grab a cup of coffee and a chocolate donut to get her past the shakiness and nausea. In a matter of minutes, her symptoms were relieved only to return again in a couple of hours.

A friend suggested that she try a tablespoon of honey at bedtime. It seemed crazy, but she took the advice. In a matter of days, she began to notice significant changes. She was no longer awakened with the intense nausea, shakiness, and malaise. She now felt like eating a good breakfast and seemed to get through the day to an early lunch without experiencing any symptoms. She also began taking "honey sticks" to work for use when the workload kept her at her desk. In less than a few weeks, she pronounced herself cured and symptom free, thanks to a bit of honey before bedtime.

When she retired in the fall of 2008, Becky remarked that she owed her longevity on the job to honey!

UNMASKING THE PRETENDERS: THE FACTS ABOUT ARTIFICIAL SWEETENERS

The headlines are eye catching:
"New Sweetener Approved with No Calories, No Carbohydrates"
"FDA-Approved Sweetener–Safe for Diabetics"

The tag lines are equally impressive:
"...all-natural sweetener that looks exactly like honey, tastes exactly like honey, and has the same consistency as honey. *In fact, it's putting bees out of business.*"
and
"Made from sugar so it tastes like sugar."

Marketing is all about perception. It is no mistake that the marketing of various artificial sweeteners attempts to change perceptions, to make something seem to be something that it is not. Another way of making this point is to ask the question "When is a carbohydrate not a carbohydrate?" Answer: "When it is called by a different name and defined in different terms." The companies that manufacture artificial sweeteners have been at this for years, at least since the 1950s when such substances were first approved for human consumption.

There are over 20 natural sugar substitutes and about 10 artificial sweeteners that have been identified and produced in the past 40 years. A few of the better-known products have captured the market share for artificial sweeteners in the United States.[54] Many who are concerned about their weight or who are diabetic or pre-diabetic use artificial sweeteners almost exclusively, as most physicians recommend this substitution. Some even buy "sugar-free" honey from one of the big box stores thinking that it is a good substitute for sugar. Those who are disciplined about following this advice often become frustrated with their inability to lose weight. Many find that their blood sugar levels continue to swing widely throughout the day and are elevated in the early morning hours in spite of having had nothing to eat since the night before.

Recent studies have begun to point out an alarming observation. Weight gain, rather than weight loss, is associated with the consumption of some sugar substitutes. Many of these products have significant glycemic load. Others result in a pronounced insulin effect in spite of the fact that they contain no sugar nor do they raise blood sugar levels.

The problem with artificial sweeteners is that they fool the brain. The instant the sweetness receptors on the tongue sense that something sweet (whatever the source) is being ingested, the brain is alerted. In turn, the pancreas begins to release insulin. This "gustatory (or taste-initiated) insulin response" in the absence of any actual caloric intake has the same effect on blood sugar as if a high caloric load were being consumed.

Increased insulin levels drive circulating blood sugar into the cells, where it is converted to glycogen and/or stored as fat. Blood sugar levels drop and appetite hormones are released, prompting hunger and the need for more food ingestion leading to a greater risk of weight gain and obesity.

"Sugar-free" honey is another story. This product is not honey at all but an adulterated syrup blend sweetened with maltitol, a sugar alcohol that is a disaccharide (made up of two different sugars). Maltitol has an effect on blood sugar levels similar to sugar, and its caloric load is similar to sucrose.

In addition, its larger molecular structure means that it is not absorbed in the upper part of the small intestine like sugar or honey but passes into the large intestine. Here, it is partially metabolized to form triglycerides, or fatty acids, which then contribute to elevated lipids and increased fat deposits throughout the body. Maltitol also produces undesirable digestive tract consequences including excess gas and bloating.

The process of determining the usefulness or healthfulness of these sugar substitutes, whether natural or artificial, should include an understanding of the effects of these substances on the body. This is critical, as use of these sugar substitutes has mushroomed within the "diet-food" industry. Medical and health professionals have also recommended them for persons with glucose metabolism impairments and diabetes.

Are they beneficial for weight loss? Do they help lower blood sugar levels in diabetics? In summary, it can be safely said that diet drinks (and any foods containing artificial sweeteners for that matter), in spite of their lower calorie status, may play a significant role in causing fat formation and storage by way of their gustatory insulin effect. In fact, similar metabolic hazards (increased prevalence of the metabolic syndrome,[55] higher risk of obesity,[56, 57] high blood pressure, and diabetes mellitus[58]) are more common in individuals consuming many of these sugar substitutes. *Given the fact that some artificial sweeteners are metabolized directly to triglycerides, and others stimulate insulin release, it is not surprising that diabetic patients and dieters using these products continue to have elevated serum triglycerides, store more fat, and continue to gain weight.*

The Dieter's Dilemma

(Adapted from *The Honey Revolution – Abridged*)

J anice, Barb, and Ann worked in the same office. They were all somewhat overweight, constantly dieting, and all equally unsuccessful in losing weight in spite of constant effort. Each day, they collectively consumed numerous diet soft drinks with the hope of limiting calories and shedding a few pounds. Each month, they found themselves in need of wardrobe expansions.

An office associate suggested that they abandon their diet drinks and start drinking regular soda. The three agreed to follow the advice, incredible as it may have seemed.

More unbelievable than the advice, however, were the results that began to manifest themselves in a matter of three to four weeks. Each of the three women reported significant weight loss, ranging from four to six pounds. Unable to explain the results except for the elimination of diet sodas, their collective experiences reinforced what researchers have known for some time. The regular consumption of artificially sweetened beverages is associated with more weight gain, more fat accumulation around the midsection, elevated fatty acids in the blood, as well as increased risks for obesity and elevated blood lipids.

The reason for this is quite simple: Receptors on the tongue alert the brain that an incoming sweet load is being ingested. (The sweetness receptors on the tongue do not differentiate between artificial and natural sweeteners.) A signal from the brain then triggers the pancreas to release insulin even though no calories are actually being consumed. Insulin drives the existing circulating blood sugar into the cells where it is stored as fat. Thus, dieters who try to avoid calories by drinking diet soft drinks gain weight.

Most artificial sweeteners trigger what is referred to as the "gustatory insulin response." The release of insulin leads to a precipitous drop in blood sugar, which prompts the release of appetite-stimulating hormones, increasing food ingestion and weight gain over time.

This is exactly the phenomenon experienced by our three dieters and by countless others who follow their doctor's advice to use artificial sweeteners as a means of limiting calories and losing weight. Better to take a bit of honey and maintain a stable blood sugar than experience the yo-yo effect common to many dieters who depend on artificial sweeteners.

HONEY: NATURE'S AMAZING MEDICINE

*"**Honey**, butter, sheep, and cheese for David and those who were with him. For they said, 'You must all be very tired and hungry and thirsty after your long march through the wilderness.'" (2 Samuel 17: 29, New Living Translation)*

Medicinal Uses of Honey in the Recorded History of Many Cultures*

2100 - 2000 B.C. – The Sumerians mixed river dust with honey and oil to treat infected skin ulcers – a prescription written on clay tablets.

About 2000 B.C. – The Egyptians used honey to treat open wounds.

1800 B.C. – The Babylonians used honey in medicine and referred to it in the Code of Hammurabi.

1400 B.C. – Sustra, a surgeon from India wrote of the medicinal properties of eight different honey varietals.

1200 B.C. – Charak, another Indian physician regarded honey as a tonic and a mild laxative.

230 A.D. – Athenaeus from Ancient Greece wrote that all who ate honey and bread for breakfast "were free from disease all their lives."

About 650 A.D. – Ibn Magih, from the Arab-Muslim culture quoted from Mohammed in writing "honey is a remedy for every illness."

600 - 700 AD – The Chinese mixed honey with opium as a therapeutic relief for pain.

1759 – The first English book on honey was published by Sir John Hill. "The Virtues of Honey in Preventing many of the worst Disorders, and in the Certain Cure of Several others . . ."

[* From *Honey A Comprehensive Survey*, edited by Eva Crane, MSc, PhD, Crane, Russak & Company, Inc., New York, Printed in Great Britain, 1975]

As with most health related discussions, the perspective of the writer is important. Throughout this book, and in this chapter in particular, I am writing from the vantage point of a medical doctor. What is about to be discussed is not rooted in alternative medicine, naturopathy, apicultural practices, folklore, or other non-traditional approaches to healthcare.[59] What follows is based on credible research and scientific evidence, evidence that is both predictable and reproducible.

Admittedly, some of the evidence comes from small research studies using animals or humans conducted on a short-term observational basis, that is, they are not randomized, controlled, double-blind, peer-reviewed studies utilizing large populations with data collected over months or years, all factors considered to be the *sine qua non* of most scientific research conducted in the United States.[60] Some of what follows has its origins in non-Western medical practice and research. Western medicine and particularly medicine as practiced in the United States is rather slow to adopt practices and traditions that originate elsewhere.

Nevertheless, it appears safe at this juncture to assert that *honey is nature's amazing medicine*. That statement may defy modern conventional wisdom. Many of the benefits of consuming honey occur over several days, weeks, months or even years in some cases. This may not be good news for a generation hooked on quick fixes, instant cures, immediate gratification and a "can't-I-just-take-a-pill-for-it-Doc?" mentality.

The health benefits, some might say "therapeutic" qualities of honey, can be attributed to four fairly distinct mechanisms of action. A fifth category has been added to include the benefits of honey that do not conveniently fit within the first four. While the mechanisms of action within each category are distinct, there is significant overlap among the categories, which will be pointed out. The categories are:

- The metabolic benefits,
- The benefits associated with improvement in quality of sleep,
- The effects on the immune system,
- The antimicrobial benefits, and
- The miscellaneous health benefits.

The *metabolic benefits* of consuming honey are derived from its primary constituents and how they are metabolized and stored in the body as described earlier. In addition, honey contains many trace ingredients that act as antioxidants. Honey consumption has an anti-inflammatory effect on the cells and tissues of the body even though the same sugars contained in honey, when consumed independently as glucose, sucrose or HFCS have the opposite effect.

The metabolic benefits of consuming honey and the benefits associated with *improvement in the quality of sleep* gained by eating honey just before bedtime overlap significantly. In other words, the metabolic benefits of honey are evidenced at nighttime during sleep, as well as during the day. The effect is the same around the clock. However, it is the reduction of metabolic stress during sleep that results in an improvement in the quality of sleep. Improved quality of sleep is itself a factor associated with a reduction of the risk of various conditions and diseases, and therefore these benefits will be considered separately.

The effects of honey on the immune system may relate to its antioxidant and anti-inflammatory properties. In addition, there are research conclusions that suggest that honey facilitates the ability of tumor cells to destroy themselves,[61] thus inhibiting the growth of certain cancer cells. Other research that reports enhanced immune system parameters from the consumption of honey state no specific mechanisms of action to explain the observations.

Its antimicrobial (or antibiotic) benefits have been the most studied health benefit of honey within the past few years. Research study design is relatively straightforward in these cases as most studies can be done in a laboratory where honey's effect on bacterial, fungal, or viral growth can be observed and compared with other substances including existing antibiotics. Clinical research on the efficacy of honey in the treatment of skin infections, skin ulcers, and in treatment of burns has advanced at an accelerated pace. Multiple honey varietals have been studied from several countries, and though the evidence shows large variation in the antimicrobial activity of natural honeys, there is general consensus among most studies that honey has remarkable therapeutic potential.

The miscellaneous benefits of honey include its use as a natural fuel for exercise. In addition, the benefits of honey related to conditions associated with aging will be presented.

THE METABOLIC BENEFITS OF CONSUMING HONEY

"Eat honey, dear child–it's good for you." (Proverbs 24:13, The Message)

M*etabolic actions* relate to how a substance is digested, absorbed, stored, and utilized or metabolized within the human system. The mechanisms of action of honey (how and why it does what it does) depend to a large degree on the specific constituents of honey. In addition, there are antioxidant and anti-inflammatory properties of honey that affect cells, tissues and organs within the body in positive ways.

Previously, honey has been described as consisting primarily of fructose and glucose in a near 1:1 ratio, along with other substances which affect the release of insulin from the pancreas. It is these factors that allow honey to be rapidly digested, absorbed into the blood, and carried to the liver, where it is converted directly into liver glycogen. Because of this rather simple action, honey is most effective in its role in combating weight gain and obesity, the first of several medical conditions and diseases discussed that can be affected, improved or eliminated altogether by adopting a simple strategy of consuming honey regularly.

Perhaps it need not be stated, but moderation in all things still seems to be sound advice. Following one of my presentations on honey and health, my wife and I joined members of the audience in the cafeteria for lunch. As we began to eat, a rather portly (obese) gentleman asked if he could join us. He placed his *two* trays of food on the table across from us, each containing multiple plates piled high with pasta, rolls, deserts, etc. "Doc," he announced loudly, " I have decided to take your advice. Before I left my room I had my two table-spoons of honey. Do you think it will work for me?" Somehow there must have been something missed in the translation.

This health benefit of consuming honey versus refined sugar or HFCS may take weeks, months, or even years to be fully revealed. In humans, studies that compare dietary variations and their effect on weight typically involve lengthy rigorous protocols with large populations. Animal studies conducted over shorter periods of time have shown significant weight reduction among the subjects fed honey rather than sugar. Randomized controlled studies that compare honey-based diets to diets containing sugar or HFCS would take years to complete, which explains in part why there are no such studies on which to report. Retrospective studies would be nearly impossible due to the fact that identifying a population not exposed to sugar or HFCS to serve as control groups would be difficult. It is encouraging, however, to note that research considering the metabolic benefits of honey is increasing, as are the health benefits experienced by many.

Honey for Weight Gain and Obesity

The regular consumption of honey and the elimination of excessive sugar and HFCS from your diet require a definite change of habits, especially given the fact that 20% of today's under-18 population are obese, and two thirds of adults are overweight or obese. There is little doubt that the epidemic of obesity we are now witnessing in the United States has its roots in habits formed at an early age.

Honey-fed animals, compared with other animals fed predominately sucrose (table sugar) over a period of several months, had up to 22% *less weight gain.*[62] In rat years, this translates into an age related to mid-life for humans. If the extrapolation of data from rats to humans has merit, and you could infer that it does, the metabolic effects of honey consumption may take a while to manifest themselves with regard to weight gain and obesity. It makes sense to begin a honey strategy early.

Short-term human observational studies have provided additional evidence and scientific data to support the use of honey in patients who are obese.[63] Other findings indicate that test subjects eating honey *for only four weeks* had lower total cholesterol, lower LDL-cholesterol, lower triglycerides, lower fasting blood sugar, and lower C-reactive protein (CRP) while at the same time showing a *small reduction in body weight and total body fat.*[64] Though you would not think of honey consumption as the first line of defense against obesity, it might be well to note that hundreds of people have reported some weight loss following the incorporation of honey into their diets.

One important anecdotal observation is that as honey consumption increases and is sustained over time, your craving for sweets will diminish. This is good news for those hooked on sugar. There is no downside to the substitution of honey for sugar or HFCS, and the benefits could be enormous, even *revolutionary*.

Honey for Diabetes

There have been countless times in the past few years after speaking about the health benefits of honey that someone will soundly object by saying, "Oh, I can't eat honey. I have diabetes. My doctor has told me to avoid all sweets." Such, unfortunately, is the state of knowledge about honey among the general public and among most health professionals.

Rather than arming patients with facts to refute the apparent ignorance of their health care professional – a tactic bound to fail – a better strategy is suggested. Diabetic patients should simply ask their doctor if fruits are permitted in their diets. Since the question is a bit rhetorical, they can have confidence in knowing that honey is permitted. A tablespoon of honey consists of nearly the same carbohydrate (glucose – fructose) content as a medium-sized apple. The diabetic patient can also be assured that consuming honey will produce a significantly lower blood sugar response than an equivalent amount of sugar or glucose rich starches.[65, 66]

Previously, we have shown how honey consumption regulates blood sugar, reducing high blood sugar levels and preventing low blood sugar. Observational studies have shown us that honey consumption produces a significantly lower elevation in blood sugar levels compared to equal ingested doses of sucrose or glucose. Regular honey consumption results in lower average blood sugar levels (10 to 20 mg% or more) and in lower HbA_{1c} levels (0.2 to 0.4%). Over a few weeks or months, honey consumption will produce lower HbA_{1c}

levels in individuals who are pre-diabetic or have full-blown diabetes. In fact, the more advanced your intolerance for glucose, the better you will tolerate honey. This seems counter-intuitive given that honey is nearly equal parts glucose and fructose.

After ingestion, honey is rapidly absorbed and converted into glycogen in the liver, thus removing glucose from the circulation and lowering blood sugar levels. Lower blood sugar levels mean a lessened demand for and release of insulin, thus accounting for a stabilization of blood sugar within the circulation. Logic would dictate that the addition of honey to the diet, along with the elimination of most sugar and HFCS, should be the first recommended treatment of choice for type 2 diabetes.[67, 68, 69] Honey may also be recommended for patients with type 1 diabetes as recent studies have shown positive effects from the long-term consumption of honey in those individuals.[70, 71]

The reason that honey consumption results in less insulin being produced and released from the pancreas may be related to *compounds contained in honey that regulate the production of hepatic insulin sensitizing substance (HISS) in the liver*. Though this hypothesis remains to be confirmed in research, it is known that eating honey results in a lesser insulin release than what occurs following ingestion of sucrose or HFCS.

How much honey is enough for individuals with diabetes? Generally, three to five tablespoons of honey a day is sufficient. A good regimen to follow is to consume a tablespoon of honey in the morning with fruit or yogurt. This will immediately begin to stock the liver glycogen reserve that has been depleted throughout the night. Another tablespoon or two should be consumed at bedtime. This will help to "top off" the tank that fuels the brain during the night and prevent the release of cortisol and adrenalin from the adrenal glands. During the day and depending on your activity level, another one or two tablespoons can be ingested with fruit snacks, in baked goods, or as used in cooking. If you are sedentary most of the day, and have no regular exercise program, the evening and morning doses should be sufficient.

Honey contains about 60 calories per tablespoon. The percentage of your total caloric requirements provided from simple sugars should not exceed 10%. Thus, the 180 to 300 calories a day provided from honey is sufficient, unless excessive energy demands allow for additional consumption.

The amount of honey that can be given safely to children with diabetes depends on weight of the child and his/her activity levels. The honey dosage for adults assumes an average weight of 170 pounds, so if a child weighs only one forth as much, the honey dose should be reduced accordingly.

There is one potential caution regarding honey for diabetes that should be mentioned. Some honey varietals contain excessively high levels of a compound called methylglyoxal (MGO), such as Manuka honey discussed in the section on the antimicrobial benefits of honey.

Manuka honey is produced from nectar from the flower of a plant native to New Zealand's North Island and portions of southeast Australia. Manuka honey is a true mono-floral honey, made by bees that forage from just one species, *Leptospermum scoparium*, which blooms for just two to six weeks a year, thus making Manuka honey quite expensive to produce and export. It is typically found in health food stores and specialty food shops in the U.S. (It should be noted also that some honey labeled Manuka honey may be generic or blended honey, so labeled to capitalize on the known healthful benefits of Manuka honey.)

Manuka honey is noted for its powerful antibiotic activity, primarily due to its MGO content. The unfortunate fact is that MGO is highly toxic to the cells within the human body. Because MGO is so toxic to cells, rapid detoxification is necessary and the process of detoxification results in a significant negative side effect, producing the same metabolites that result from intracellular oxidative stress due to hyperglycemia in patients with diabetes.[72] These metabolites, when attached to receptors found on cells from the lung, liver, kidney or blood, contribute to age- and diabetes-related chronic inflammatory diseases such as atherosclerosis, asthma, arthritis, myocardial infarction, kidney disease, retinopathy, and other conditions of the nervous system.[73, 74, 75]

In addition, other research findings published in 2006 indicate that MGO is also associated with the early phases of insulin resistance. Even short exposures to MGO can lead to an inhibition of insulin-induced signaling. Thus, "methylglyoxal may not only induce the debilitating complications of diabetes but may also contribute to the pathophysiology of diabetes in general."[76] In other words, MGO not only contributes to increased oxidative stress within the cells of the body by its rapid metabolism into AGEs, but also may be one of the causative factors of diabetes by its inhibition of insulin.

Many honey varietals may contain some MGO, especially honey that has been heated. In fact, some European countries test honey specifically for MGO and ban honey imports with higher levels of MGO. Fortunately, the amount of MGO is small or absent in most honey varietals. Honey containing large amounts of MGO, such as Manuka honey, may be safely used as a topical agent for treating superficial skin infections, wounds and burns. Before consuming Manuka honey, you should consider the facts above, especially if you are diabetic, have abnormalities with blood sugar metabolism, or have experienced early stages of insulin resistance.

Duane's Story
(Adapted from *The Honey Revolution – Abridged*)

D uane was in his 50s when his doctor diagnosed diabetes. He wasn't particularly overweight, but a sedentary lifestyle as a pastor and counselor, combined with irregular eating habits, had taken its toll. After his diagnosis, he became "religious" about monitoring his blood sugar levels, sometimes three to four times a day, and keeping accurate records. Modest dietary changes and medication seemed to help control his numbers, yet over time his blood sugar averages began to creep up again.

Nearing the age of 70, Duane found his blood sugar averages running 10 to 15 mg% higher than his target range, especially in the morning upon awakening. His HbA_{1c} level was acceptable at 6.1%, though he wanted to see it lower. His physician brother-in-law suggested that a tablespoon of honey consumed before bedtime could bring his numbers down and boldly predicted that his next HbA_{1c} would be down by 0.2 to 0.4%.

The advice seemed counterintuitive ("Eating sugar before bedtime to *lower* blood sugar?"), yet he was up for the challenge. Duane began taking honey before retiring for the night. After three weeks of consistently downing a tablespoon of honey before bed, Duane reported that his morning blood sugar levels were averaging 10 to 15 mg% lower, and his blood sugar averages throughout the day were stabilizing within a normal range.

Anticipating his next checkup in a month, he was encouraged to stay the course and make no other changes in his diet. His next doctor's visit confirmed the prediction: Duane's HbA$_{1c}$ report came back at 5.8%, a reduction of 0.3%. Nothing else had changed in his diet or lifestyle routine except for the addition of a table-spoon of honey before bedtime.

Duane's story is not unique. Anecdotal accounts from countless individuals across varying age groups have repeated his story. The simple addition of a table-spoon of honey consumed before bedtime results in the stabilization of blood sugar levels within a normal range. This experience has been consistent without regard to medication being taken. Furthermore, the positive results seem to be more pronounced in individuals with more severe glucose intolerance.

Honey for Cardiovascular Disease

There is growing evidence and scientific data to support the use of honey, not only in patients with diabetes, lipid abnormalities, and obesity but also with cardiovascular disease.[77] Second only to the positive effects on blood sugar and lipids within the body are the protective and beneficial effects of honey on the heart and blood vessels.

The human heart never sleeps; it must always recover "on the fly." Because of this, the most potent risk factor for heart disease is chronic exposure to increased levels of the stress hormones cortisol and adrenalin (resulting from metabolic stress). Increased levels of adrenalin increase heart rate and blood pressure. Elevated cortisol levels over time cause hypertension, arrhythmia, stroke, and atherosclerosis. Cortisol also inhibits the action of insulin, meaning that glucose is kept in the circulating blood rather than passing quickly into the heart muscle cells where it can be used for energy. Honey consumption reduces chronic metabolic stress during rest, thus reducing the stress on the heart while it is recovering during the nighttime.

Honey is known to reduce the risk factors for cardiovascular disease by inhibiting inflammation, improving function of the lining of blood vessels, lowering blood lipids, and increasing the resistance to oxidation of low-density lipoproteins (such as LDL-cholesterol).[78] In another study, researchers found that honey consumption, compared to sucrose, lowered the risk factors for cardiovascular disease in healthy patients as well as in patients with elevated risk factors.[79] The risk factors lowered by consuming honey included total cholesterol, triglycerides, LDL cholesterol, fasting blood sugar, and C-reactive protein (CRP). In addition, HDL (or good) cholesterol was increased. These results were seen in test subjects that consumed 70 grams (about 3 ½ tablespoons) of honey per day for 30 days.

Honey also possesses potent antioxidant and anti-inflammatory activity that positively affects cardiovascular disease due to a wide range of compounds including flavonoids or polyphenols (which have properties of antioxidants), peptides, organic acids, and enzymes. It is these substances that are believed by many to provide healthful benefits for the heart and blood vessels.

Some investigators have found that the antioxidant levels in honey are very pronounced. They assert that it is this total antioxidant capacity as well as the presence of substantial quantities of minerals and nitric oxide (which relaxes blood vessels) in honey that are directly responsible for the cardio-protective effects caused by adrenalin-induced heart disorders and blood vessel dysfunction.[80]

Another study found that the consumption of natural unprocessed honey for only 15 days decreased the levels of hormones in the body (prostaglandins, and prostaglandin-like substances) that cause inflammation.[81] These substances actually suppress certain immune system functions and lead to atherosclerosis, the underlying cause of cardiovascular disease.

One additional way that honey consumption reduces the risk of heart disease is by its effect on homocysteine (HCY). HCY is the normal by-product of the metabolism of the amino acid, methionine. The accumulation of HCY is associated with an increased risk of heart disease[82] and about ten percent of coronary deaths each year are attributed to high HCY levels. Honey consumption significantly lowers HCY in the body.[83]

These are stunning examples of how a simple strategy of regular honey consumption can positively affect the diseases of the heart and blood vessels. The mechanisms of action (how honey accomplishes this) are varied and can be summarized as follows:

- Honey reduces the levels of stress hormones, allowing the heart to recover "on-the-fly."
- Honey contains antioxidants that protect the heart against stress hormone-induced disorders and blood vessel dysfunction.
- Honey reduces inflammation, thus improving the function of the lining of blood vessels and reducing the risk of atherosclerosis or "hardening of the arteries."
- Honey lowers several risk factors associated with heart and blood vessel disease.
- Honey lowers substances in the body known to cause ten percent of heart attack deaths each year.

Eric's Story
(Adapted from *The Honey Revolution – Abridged*)

E ric was lying beside the mountain path at 8,300 feet elevation when the search and rescue team found him. He had gone for a hike that morning and was making his descent when he felt a sharp stabbing pain in his left shoulder. He had a hard time catching his breath, rested for a moment and tried to continue downward to the trailhead where his car was parked. When the pain resumed with what seemed to be constricting pressure over his mid chest area, he had clarity enough to abandon his descent, call 911 on his cell phone, give his location and wait for help.

Eric was 69. In earlier years he was a marathon runner (he had completed over 30 marathons) and in midlife had taken up mountain biking and hiking. He was not overweight, but closer inspection revealed a midsection flabbiness that seemed inconsistent with his muscular legs and trim upper body. He had no history of heart disease.

The cardiac monitor in the ambulance on the way to the emergency room showed acute and dramatic changes. Fortunately for Eric, he reached the hospital, and was immediately admitted to the electro-physiology cardiac lab. Three stints were placed in one coronary artery which was effectively 100% occluded, and another stint was placed in another artery that showed 70% occlusion. Eric survived, but questions lingered.

Eric's story reminds me of the first-person commercials you see on TV for Bayer aspirin. The couple is sitting on the couch and the very fit-looking husband says, "I was in perfect health and out of the blue I had a heart attack." How can you explain coronary artery occlusion (heart attack) in an otherwise seasoned runner and avid exerciser in supposedly perfect health? The answer is predictable though not widely understood within a context of conventional wisdom.

There can be only one explanation, which also informs us why over 50% of those suffering heart attacks have normal cholesterol measurements. For many, fats, or being fat, are not the problem underlying the acute onset of heart disease like Eric's. Metabolic stress, underscored by chronic or repeated release of elevated levels of cortisol and adrenalin due to brain starvation (the hallmark of the metabolic syndrome) is the problem.

That indeed was Eric's case. Here is how it began. Eric was a brilliant mathematician and academician. He taught at a prestigious military academy. He was driven in his pursuit of excellence in his teaching and personal life, which meant he was early to work, late to leave, frequently skipped meals, especially breakfast, snacked on junk food and consumed large amounts of coffee throughout the day and then wound down by taking long runs or bike rides without proper fueling before or after.

He didn't sleep well and frequently awakened between 3:00 and 4:00 AM unable to get back to sleep for 45 minutes to an hour, only to be awakened by his alarm at 5:30 AM so that he could arrive for work before

7:30 AM. Breakfast, if he took the time to gulp it down, consisted of cereal or toast and coffee. Once at work, the coffee was free and donuts and pastries were readily available throughout the morning, which seemed to keep him going. Lunch, when he could take time for it, was hurried and overloaded with starch or carbohydrates which rapidly increased his blood sugar, only to be followed by excessive insulin release and a subsequent rapidly falling blood glucose leaving him hungry again by mid afternoon. Again, coffee and snacks satisfied temporarily until supper.

He seldom ate fruit, but consumed large amounts of vegetables in season that he grew in his garden. He didn't eat much red meat, avoided fatty foods, and consumed low-fat options when he could. He avoided any food before bedtime that he believed would only be unnecessary energy during sleep and would only turn to fat. He assumed his diet was heart healthy (despite the donuts) never once considering that his diet was at the heart of his heart problem.

Eric was experiencing metabolic stress for more than 18 to 20 hours of every day. His brain was silently monitoring its fuel reserve in the liver and found it wanting. From nearly 10:00 PM every evening until shortly after lunch, no liver glycogen was available directly from food intake. The brain had no recourse but to manufacture it from amino acids available from muscle protein. His long periods of exercise, experienced three to five times a week, were undertaken with depleted liver glycogen stores, further driving metabolic stress and muscle protein cannibalism just to fuel his hungry brain.

When he did eat, his carbohydrate consumption succeeded in raising his blood sugar temporarily, only to be followed by an excessive release of insulin. In 90 to

120 minutes, he was still left with little liver glycogen to fuel his brain during the night.

Fortunately, good genetics had protected Eric from obesity, early onset of diabetes, and other conditions and diseases on the metabolic stress continuum. But good genes could not protect Eric from decades of metabolic stress directed at his cardiovascular system, and on approaching the beginning of his eighth decade of life, it finally caught up with him.

The good news is that Eric's heart attack did not end his life. He was given a reprieve. A change in diet, which included proper fueling before and after exercise and before bedtime, promised to give Eric many more productive years of computational instruction and good health.

Honey for the Brain

An entire book in *The Honey Revolution Series* has been devoted to improving the way you can fuel your brain.[84] Honey – the gold standard of carbohydrates – is described in that book as the quintessential brain fuel as it produces more liver glycogen per gram than any other food. No other natural food is even close.

The brain uses primarily glucose for energy under normal circumstances. Given that fact, it seems reasonable that some attention be paid to how we maintain and store glucose for the brain. The human brain is an organ with a colossal demand for glucose and yet it has no internal energy supply and must depend on an external or reserve fuel supply. To ensure a constant supply of energy for itself, the brain closely monitors and regulates its fuel availability. It considers its own demands as priority one even to the extent of depriving other organs and tissues of their energy supply when it senses that its supply is running low.

The Fuel Reserve for the Brain

So where does the brain get its fuel? One source is glucose from the circulating blood (blood sugar). The average quantity of blood in the adult human system is around 5 liters, and each liter will contain around 1 gram of glucose. That means the total amount of blood sugar available at any one time is about 5 grams. That amount could provide fuel for the brain for about 1 hour assuming no other organs or tissues were consuming glucose – not a valid assumption. In actual life, the blood contains enough glucose to fuel the brain for no more than a few minutes before the blood glucose concentration drops to a dangerously low level (as in hypoglycemia). Shortly thereafter, a coma would be activated as a desperate last-resort strategy to maintain the life of the brain. Blood sugar measurement, therefore, does not give us a reliable indication of fuel availability for the brain, except in the very short term (a few minutes at best), just as water flowing from the tap is not a measure of water availability, except in the short term. The brain must have a more substantial fuel reserve for use between meals, during overnight fasting and exercise. This reserve is the liver, where glucose is stored as glycogen and released for the brain and other organs on demand.

The average capacity of this storage reserve is about 75 grams (the range may vary from 60 to 110 grams of glycogen depending on body size and other conditions of overall liver health). Given the fact that the liver will release about 10 grams of glucose per hour during rest to provide fuel for the brain, red blood cells and the kidneys, the liver glycogen reserve will provide enough fuel for the brain for 6 to 8 hours.

Foods That Fuel the Brain

Certain foods add to the liver glycogen store rather than raise blood sugar. In other words, these foods, though they contain sugars, contribute less to elevated levels of blood sugar and more to the formation of liver glycogen. By creating liver glycogen directly, these foods effectively fuel the brain. Such foods are those that contain fructose (fruit sugar) along with equal amounts of glucose, such as fruits, some vegetables, and *honey*. In other words, foods that contain a balanced or nearly equal ratio of glucose to fructose, without an excessive amount of starch, actually fill the brain fuel reserve and ensure that the brain has a continuous supply of fuel.[85] *The key here is fructose.*[86]

The Facts about Fructose

There is much conflicting talk about fructose today. Let's sort out what is true from what is exaggeration or myth. As we have indicated, fructose in the diet is essential for glucose to be taken into the liver where it is converted to glycogen and stored. Without fructose, glucose essentially bypasses the liver and raises the blood sugar level causing an insulin spike that drives glucose into the cells where it is used for energy or stored as muscle glycogen or fat. In other words, fructose is essential in its role as facilitating brain fuel storage in the liver.

Fructose is relatively worthless as a fuel for energy in the rest of the body. The muscle cells can't take it in or store it. It cannot be stored in fat cells. Except for the liver, the only other cells in the body that can take in fructose and convert it to glycogen and utilize it for energy are sperm cells, which only benefits about half the population.

In spite of its insignificance in providing fuel for nearly every cell in the body, fructose is important in the diet, especially as it relates to the provision of energy for the brain. Without it, liver glycogen is not rapidly formed, and the brain's energy reserve is not replenished.

There is, however, a big caution about fructose that must be underscored. There is a limit as to the amount of fructose that can be used by the liver at any one time. As the liver is the only organ in the body that can metabolize small quantities of fructose, excessive amounts of fructose can quickly overwhelm the liver. Once the liver glycogen store is full, no more fructose can be converted and stored as glycogen. In an attempt to get rid of excessive fructose, the liver simply breaks it down into three-carbon molecules that enter the fatty acid cycle to form triglycerides which combine to form very low density lipoproteins (VLDL) that enter the blood stream and are carried to fat cells for storage.

The *average* amount of fructose consumed by individuals in the U.S. is estimated to be in the range of 55 grams per day, with adolescents (12-18 years) consuming nearly 73 grams per day.[87] Multiple research studies have associated this level of fructose consumption with obesity, elevated triglycerides, cardiovascular disease and diabetes.[88] A recent study has shown that 74 grams of fructose a day from HFCS (the equivalent to the amount in 2 ½ cans of soft drinks or 30 ounces) is associated with high blood pressure.[89] Other comprehensive review studies are not so convincing as "on closer examination, much of the accusing evidence appears based on confusion of fructose-containing sweeteners and their compositions, incorrect reporting of fructose use and intake figures, extreme experimental designs bearing little resemblance in amount or pattern to actual human use, and emphasis on statistical rather than clinical importance."[90]

What can be agreed upon is this. *A little fructose is essential. Too much fructose is potentially extremely harmful to your health.* As the liver can only store 75 grams of glycogen at once, a good estimate of the maximum amount of fructose that should be consumed at any one time along with glucose is significantly less than half that amount or about 30 grams (the amount contained in 16 ounces of a soft drink).

A tablespoon of honey (21 grams) contains an average of 7.5 grams of glucose and 8.6 grams of fructose, equivalent to the amounts found in one medium sized apple. This amount of fructose and glucose would result in the formation of about 17 grams of liver glycogen. Two tablespoons of honey would result in the formation of between 30 to 35 grams of liver glycogen, just the right amount to "top-off" the liver glycogen reserve at bedtime or between meals.

This modest amount presents a stark contrast to what happens when you consume a soft drink from your local convenience store. A 32-ounce soft drink contains over 75 grams of fructose alone, forcing the liver to metabolize the excess fructose into fatty acids. The additional amount of glucose is basically a sugar blast that raises blood sugar and initiates a massive insulin spike which drives the excess glucose into the muscle and fat cells were it is stored as fat, making it unavailable for the brain.

The 13 (Often Ignored) Principles of Fueling the Brain

The preceding information underscores a few key principles of brain fueling that merit restating. They are listed in numerical order, but such listing implies no particular priority. Here they are:

1. Brain (or cerebral) hunger is the driving force behind obesity, diabetes, and all of the conditions and diseases associated with the metabolic syndrome.
2. The brain has no primary fuel reserve of its own and without fuel delivered from the circulating blood, brain cells would barely survive 30 seconds.
3. The brain uses glucose as its primary source of energy. The brain will burn amino acids from proteins and some lactic acid (lactate) but both of these fuels are in short or transient supply in the circulation. Only under limited circumstances does the brain burn fats for energy, such as in the latter stages of

starvation, and only after blood glucose and liver glycogen stores are exhausted.

4. Though the brain uses glucose as its primary source of energy, *excessive* glucose consumption (or consumption of foods that are immediately converted to glucose in the digestive process such as starchy foods) will not result in adequate brain fueling.

5. Circulating blood sugar is limited (5 to 5½ grams at any given time) and can only provide enough fuel for the brain for 30 minutes or less.

6. The liver is the primary fuel source and active fuel reserve for the brain.

7. The liver forms glycogen from fructose and glucose when these two sugars are ingested together. (The liver also forms glycogen from left over lactic acid or lactate from muscles, but this supply is limited. Some glycogen is also produced from amino acids.)

8. When the liver glycogen supply is running low, the liver signals the brain of an impending fuel crisis.

9. The brain responds to this signal by initiating a form of metabolic stress, releasing adrenalin and cortisol from the adrenal glands. Cortisol is responsible for the breakdown of protein into amino acids that are then carried back to the liver where new glucose is formed (gluconeogenesis). Adrenalin triggers the release of glycogen from the liver, increases the heart rate and raises blood pressure, insuring that circulation to the liver and brain is maintained.

10. *Metabolic stress* is part of the brain's normal strategy to ensure its own fuel supply first.
11. The brain is a greedy taskmaster, competing for fuel resources with the rest of the body.
12. Factors such as obesity (increased body mass), high levels of lipids in the blood, chronically elevated blood sugar levels, glucose intolerance, and insulin resistance increase the metabolic demand on the body and further deplete the fuel resources needed by the brain for survival.
13. Consuming foods that have a balance of fructose and glucose (fruits, some vegetables, and honey) fuels your brain first by allowing for the direct formation of liver glycogen.

Understanding and applying these principles is critical not only for improved health and the reversal of disease progression but also for prevention of disease. The consequences of failure to fuel the brain properly can be viewed as a continuum that begins with the immediate or short-term consequences and progresses over time to ultimately involve longer-term risks. Metabolic stress is a specialized form of stress mediated by the brain to ensure its own energy supply, while at the same time affecting almost every organ of our bodies. Metabolic stress is something we do to ourselves. We can't blame it on genetics, although the ultimate result of metabolic stress or the degree to which you are affected by it may be determined by your genes. It may be triggered by external environmental or social factors or by internal emotions, but its primary cause is failure to properly provide fuel for the brain.

It's not too late to get started. Your health depends on it.

The Metabolic Stress Continuum

Metabolic stress is the direct result of poor choices that we make, typically involving lifestyle, food, nutrition, what we eat and when we eat it. It is real. It is not accidental. It is internal. It happens. *Most of us experience metabolic stress from time to time, and over 25% of us have medical conditions associated with it.* The prevalence of these conditions increases with age. The key organs involved in short-term metabolic stress are the liver and the brain. Long-term consequences involve nearly every organ in the body.

If we were to picture the conditions related to metabolic stress as a continuum shown in the inverted triangle that follows, metabolic stress would occupy the position at the lower portion of the inverted triangle. Above metabolic stress, in ascending order of significance, would be all the conditions associated with glucose intolerance including weight gain, insulin resistance, and elevations in triglycerides and other lipids. Above insulin resistance is the metabolic syndrome, type 2 diabetes, hypertension, and serum cholesterol and triglyceride elevations. Finally, listed are a host of other chronic inflammatory diseases associated with age and diabetes including cardiovascular disease, hypertension, thyroid diseases, and neuro-degenerative conditions including Alzheimer's disease, various forms of dementia, and Parkinsonism.

Describing the symptoms and conditions in this way is not meant to communicate that the levels or categories indicated by this progression are distinct. Rather, the boundaries between the levels are overlapping as one ascends from the bottom to the top. All the conditions and diseases, however, are linked to a common metabolic cause.

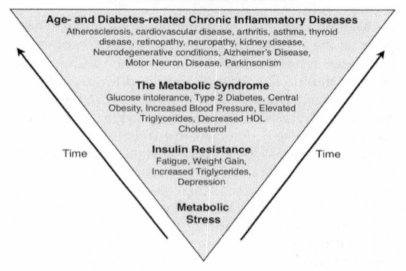

Furthermore, viewing metabolic stress as a continuum is not meant to imply that the conditions or diseases are progressive in a linear sense, that is, you must first experience a clinical condition or disease on a lower level of the diagram before you contract a clinical condition or disease on a level above, though such may be the case. It must be pointed out again that your genetic code and lifestyle may play a significant role in determining the extent to which you are possibly afflicted by the conditions and diseases of this metabolic stress continuum.

When viewing the continuum from a therapeutic or clinical point of view, it is interesting to observe that treatment interventions are usually begun at the upper levels of the triangle rather than at the lower causative level. Yet interventions begun at the level of causation (metabolic stress) may be more effective in terms of limiting morbidity or preventing the progression of future conditions or diseases.

Metabolic stress is internal physiologic stress. It happens as the result of activation of a cascade of stress hormones from the hypothalamus, the pituitary and adrenal glands (the hypothalamus-pituitary-adrenal or HPA axis). The action of the HPA axis triggers the release of adrenal stress hormones also known as glucocorticoids. These hormones are adrenalin and cortisol, sometimes referred to as "fight or flight" hormones, but they should be more correctly referred to as neuro-protective hormones because their essential purpose is to ensure that the brain has adequate fuel for functioning at all times, especially during times of physical stress. We refer to this reflex as neuro-protective, for without it the brain would quickly lapse into coma and cease functioning. It is precisely because of the small fuel reserve in the liver and in the circulating blood that this fight or flight reflex is so important to survival.

Though the glycogen storage capacity of skeletal muscle is more than ten times that of the liver, muscle glycogen is not shared. Once glucose enters the muscle cells and forms glycogen, it stays there and is not available for use by the rest of the body. Only glycogen from the liver is available for other organs and tissues. This fact is often lost on those who consider total glycogen storage capacity (liver and skeletal muscle glycogen) as a single fuel source for metabolic needs of the body.

In addition to the specific conditions and diseases of the metabolic syndrome as currently defined, we can also include many sleep disorders, hypothyroid conditions, and neuro-degenerative diseases in this progression of conditions whose etiology begins with failure to provide the brain with adequate fuel from the liver glycogen reserve.

The duration, severity, and frequency of occurrence of episodes of metabolic stress would also seem to play a role in the development of the conditions and diseases along this continuum. For some, it may take decades for disease to manifest itself. For others, only months or years. It seems that the body responds more negatively to multiple repeated insults than it may to one chronic exposure. In other words, repeated failure to fuel the brain resulting in metabolic stress night after night resulting in sleep loss may have a more significant negative effect on health than a single episode of starvation or stress from a bout of an infectious disease.

The metabolic stress continuum is interrelated with two additional closely related factors. One way of describing this interwoven relationship is as a toxic three-stranded metabolic cord comprising of the dual strands of *chronic brain starvation* and *chronic sleep loss*, described earlier, which synergistically activate the third strand of *chronic metabolic stress* mediated by the HPA axis. These three strands are so tightly interrelated, they are virtually inseparable. The binding and destructive effects of this toxic cord impact every organ system and metabolic function in the body, eventually resulting in the conditions and diseases that are collectively known as the metabolic syndrome.

Chronic starvation of the brain from inadequate liver glycogen levels night after night, year after year, drives this metabolic stress continuum contributing to sleep loss and the initiation of a profound metabolic response. The list of the conditions produced by this "toxic cord" is long and includes:

- Obesity
- Diabetes
- Heart disease

- High blood pressure
- Hyperlipidemia (elevated cholesterol and triglycerides)
- Some forms of cancer
- Osteoporosis
- Polycystic ovarian disease
- Sleep disorders including insomnia, sleep apnea
- Dementia
- Neuro-degenerative diseases including Alzheimer's Disease, Parkinsonism, and motor neuron disease (Lou Gehrig's disease)
- Depression
- Immune system compromise
- Hypothyroidism
- Arthritis
- Kidney disease
- Chronic fatigue
- Menopausal symptoms
- Infertility
- Gastrointestinal diseases
- ADHD (attention deficit hyperactivity disorder)

Prevention Must Start Early

A strategy that focuses on prevention must begin early. Children as young as 10 to 12 years old are increasingly being diagnosed with type 2 (adult-onset) diabetes. Childhood obesity is epidemic.

Alzheimer's disease, unheard of in the 1950s and 1960s, now affects one in five families. Sleep disorders have spawned a burgeoning industry of sleep clinics. Depression, ADHD, cognitive learning deficits, osteoporosis, hypothyroidism and dementia drive pharmaceutical solutions to the tune of billions of dollars annually.

The problem with *prevention* is that it requires a disciplined practice of delayed gratification. We cannot immediately see or may never see the results. It is difficult to appreciate the full effect of choices that could have eliminated many of these conditions and diseases.

Instead, our tendency is to focus on the short term, the fad diet, the quick fix, and the pill that promises to lower our numbers. We spend billions of dollars on drugs that give us a tangible sense of doing something. Our numbers (blood glucose, cholesterol, etc.) do come down, but the reality is, the underlying condition (chronic brain starvation resulting in chronic metabolic stress) may not be affected at all.

Another widespread practice of contemporary society is to accept the claims of selected, heavily marketed yet narrowly targeted foods, food supplements and additives with their pseudo-scientific health claims. We are led to believe that oatmeal and Cheerios are heart healthy and cholesterol lowering, and that low-fat yogurt is better for you. We swallow fish oil and CoQ_{10} capsules and probiotics, all in the hopes of preventing some feared medical outcome. We indulge in cleansings and purges to rid ourselves of toxins that we believe will harm us, and which, by the way, our body does a pretty good job of eliminating naturally.

All the while, our brains are starving and initiating metabolic conditions that really do kill us and deprive us of health. Our over indulgent diets are filled with sugars and carbohydrates and HFCS, which result in insulin resistance and ultimately in the metabolic syndrome and all of its associated conditions and diseases.

It all reminds me of an analogy that Jesus used in the New Testament when criticizing the hypocrisy exhibited by the teachers of the Law. "You blind guides!" he said. "You strain out a gnat but swallow a camel."[91]

Many self-proclaimed experts in nutrition and many medical professionals are blind guides. We have become so exercised in pursuing minutia ("straining out gnats") in our dietary recommendations that we sometimes lose sight of the mountain of damage we heap on ourselves and our patients by the excessive daily consumption of sugars and HFCS ("swallowing camels").

The Payoff from Proper Brain Fueling

There are three basic benefits that come from taking care of your brain's energy demands first. They are:

1. Stabilization and control of blood sugar
2. Improved sleep
3. Elimination or reduction of metabolic stress

These benefits are the result of dietary habits that keep the liver glycogen reserve maintained at all times providing energy for the brain when and how it needs it. All three are interrelated. All three are the result of a simple and inexpensive strategy that involves myth-defying choices such as eating something before bedtime.

Following nutritional guidelines based on a well intended but misguided focus on carbohydrates or calorie counting will not automatically produce these benefits. They are derived only as the result of an intentional strategy that begins and ends with liver glycogen formation from every meal or snack, a strategy never mentioned in nutritional counseling or dietary advice given to diabetics or those suffering from sleep disorders or any of the other conditions related to the metabolic syndrome.

Stabilization and Control of Blood Sugar. An adequate liver glycogen reserve means that blood sugar levels are stabilized and controlled. When blood sugar is low as during exercise or sleep, liver glycogen will be released to fuel the brain and the muscles if needed. When blood sugar is low as in reactive hypoglycemia or other forms of hypoglycemia, liver glycogen is released to increase the blood sugar level.

The ingestion of foods that form liver glycogen directly (those containing fructose and glucose in nearly equal ratios) allows for glucose to be brought into the liver to form liver glycogen. Thus, blood glucose levels do not rise as much as would be expected when consuming an equal amount of starchy foods. When blood glucose is stable and liver glycogen levels are replete, the brain is guaranteed a continuous supply of fuel.

Improved Sleep. When liver glycogen levels are maintained at optimal levels, the brain's energy needs during rest are ensured. Sleep patterns improve. Recovery sleep occurs uninterrupted throughout the night. The brain, which functions in a high energy state during rest, can count on an adequate fuel supply and will not initiate actions designed to procure fuel for itself during sleep.

Proper brain fueling before bedtime not only improves sleep patterns but also results in numerous health benefits that are the direct result of improved sleep. These range from reductions in the risks for hypertension and cardiovascular disease to improved learning and memory.

Elimination or Reduction of Metabolic Stress. When the brain is well fueled throughout the day and at night during sleep, it has no need to initiate metabolic stress. Elimination or reduction of recurrent metabolic stress is the most significant beneficial result of a well-fueled brain. The well-known risks for many conditions and diseases that are the result of chronic and repeated metabolic stress can be greatly reduced or eliminated altogether.

Jeanne's Story

J eanne weighed a scant 100 pounds when she graduated from college at age 21. At age 50 she tipped the scale at more than 150 pounds, a 50% increase in body mass. Throughout the years she complained of episodes of low blood sugar (reactive hypoglycemia her doctor called it). Her solution was to carry small containers of peanut butter or bags of nuts or portions of cheese that she consumed whenever she felt lightheaded or shaky. These did little for her early morning symptoms but did temporarily resolve her low blood sugar episodes during the day. As she got older, however, she awakened most mornings with waves of nausea and headaches. Her practice was not to eat before bedtime, believing what her mother had told her that food eaten before bed would only turn to fat. Her morning wake-ups were increasingly distressful.

What may have been a mild annoyance at age 30 now became a major challenge of midlife. It seemed that Jeanne was tired all the time. Her sleep patterns were irregular and punctuated by periods of wakefulness and restlessness. She complained of excessive daytime sleepiness, and weekends were mostly wasted just trying to catch up on rest.

She found it increasingly difficult to concentrate at times and even worried about becoming increasingly forgetful. Her doctor told her she was pre-diabetic, meaning that her blood sugar was higher than normal. Her lab tests also showed that her thyroid function was low, and her doctor wanted to put her on thyroid supplements, which, he said, would help with her chronic fatigue. Her serum calcium also was low, and she was worried about osteoporosis. Menopausal symptoms were also becoming a major challenge. Her "private summers" were distracting, unsettling, and unpredictable. It was all part of growing old, she reasoned, but she was not growing old gracefully.

Attempts to lose weight were cyclical and increasingly futile, typically resulting in short-term loss of a few pounds followed by gaining a few more. She bounced from one diet to another and even tried fasting for 12 hours a day for a time in hopes that the pounds would magically disappear. Instead, everything seemed to get worse. Her weight increased, her sleep patterns became even more irregular. Her chronic tiredness increased. Her menopausal symptoms intensified.

Sound familiar? Jeanne's story is common. She was heading for a metabolic meltdown. She faced a difficult choice – follow her doctor's advice and start taking multiple medicines designated to control her symptoms and modulate her numbers or find another way of reversing 30 years of dietary indiscretions and poor lifestyle choices.

Size really matters if you are reaching middle age weighing 50% more than you did at age 21. The reason is quite obvious. Though one's size and weight may have increased significantly with age, the liver's ability to capture and store glycogen has not. If anything, the glycogen storage capacity may decrease with age due to fatty accumulations (excess triglycerides and fatty acids) within the liver cells or liver cell destruction secondary to alcohol consumption or disease.

The need for glycogen from the liver to fuel the brain, red blood cells and kidneys, as well as a significantly increased body mass, may increase rather dramatically with age. That means that the brain is in competition with the rest of the body for the same energy store. The excess demand for glucose by a now much larger body mass may not be met by readily available glucose. This presents a problem for the brain that depends on a stable and constant energy supply.

Jeanne's meltdown came in the way of a hypertensive crisis. The emergency physician thought initially that she was having a heart attack because of her presenting chest pain. After testing and observation, it was determined that Jeanne was experiencing the results of chronic metabolic stress. Medication and rest seemed to control the symptoms for a time, and Jeanne was given a reprieve.

Honey for Menopause and Infertility

Earlier, we stated that the metabolic benefits (reduction of metabolic stress by reducing the release of adrenalin and cortisol) of consuming honey and the benefits associated with improvement in the quality of sleep resulting from eating honey just before bedtime overlap significantly. This overlap is perhaps most evident when discussing menopausal and reproductive issues. Metabolic stress occurring both during the day and during nighttime has similar effects on the reproductive systems of both males and females.

Several research studies conducted within the past few years have presented evidence of the strong links between adrenal-driven (or cortisol-driven) stress, menstrual irregularities, and both male and female infertility.[92, 93, 94, 95] These findings expand the spectrum of modern metabolic stress-driven conditions beyond what are typically included in the metabolic syndrome.

The simple strategy of consuming 1 to 2 tablespoons of honey each night before bedtime is an inexpensive and risk-free strategy to control or eliminate internal metabolic stress. By so doing, one selectively restocks the liver glycogen store for the night fast, ensures adequate provisions for the brain, and facilitates recovery physiology. The consequent reduction in adrenal stress hormones from the reduction or elimination of chronic metabolic stress ultimately improves reproductive health and facilitates optimal fertility.

Honey for Gastrointestinal Health

The influence of metabolic stress on gastrointestinal (GI) metabolism and health cannot be discounted; likewise, the relationship of insomnia and sleep disorders on a distressed GI tract cannot be discounted. Thus, GI health is another example of the overlap of the metabolic benefits of consuming honey. As shown earlier, regular honey consumption reduces metabolic stress and as we will see later, honey consumption before bedtime improves quality sleep, both benefits that improve GI function and metabolism.

Honey has also been described as a very effective probiotic,[96] meaning that it contains potentially beneficial bacteria and/or residual compounds associated with these bacteria.[97] To date, only preliminary evidence is available that associates the use of probiotics with improvement of many GI disorders such as irritable bowel syndrome, diarrhea, inflammatory bowel disease, Crohn's disease, colitis, and management of lactose intolerance. However, first-hand reports from several patients seem to confirm the fact that honey does indeed reduce bowel inflammation and can be used safely in place of sugar and other sweeteners without adverse affects.

The effectiveness of honey as an antibiotic will be discussed later. Here it is noteworthy to mention the fact that honey has been shown to kill the bacteria *H. pylori*, which is responsible for peptic ulcers, gastritis, duodenitis, and some stomach cancers. While the effectiveness of honey as an antibiotic when used systemically has not been proven, honey may be effective in killing this bacteria in the stomach and upper GI tract where concentrations would still be in the range of 3 to 5%, enough to kill most bacterial strains.

Another role for honey in promoting GI health is associated with melatonin, a hormone known to be gastro-protective. Honey ingestion before bed promotes melatonin release by way of the HYMN Cycle.[98] Melatonin opposes the actions of cortisol and serotonin, and both cortisol and serotonin adversely affect intestinal physiology when chronically overproduced. Melatonin is one of the human body's most potent antioxidants.

Clinical studies have examined the action of melatonin in gastric ulceration caused by stress, alcohol, anti-inflammatory medications, and *H. pylori* infection, and found melatonin to be protective in gastric lesions as well as a promising therapeutic agent in the control of gastric ulcerations.[99] Regular consumption of honey will prove to be an inexpensive and effective method of treating gastric ulceration simply by its effect of releasing melatonin naturally during sleep.

Honey for Thyroid Conditions

The thyroid gland is responsible for many critical functions in the body including the control of energy resources (how quickly the body uses energy), and how the body manufactures and uses proteins. Hormones produced by the thyroid regulate the growth and rate of function of many other organs and systems in the body. Many direct and indirect links exist between the thyroid and the hypothalamic-pituitary-adrenal axis (sometimes referred to as the HPA or stress axis). The thyroid even controls how sensitive the body is to other hormones produced in these glands.

Normal function of the thyroid gland can be affected by metabolic stress, the result of excessive production and release of adrenalin and cortisol. Metabolic stress, initiated during the night because of an insufficiently stocked brain fuel reserve resulting in interrupted or poor quality sleep, is also associated with abnormal thyroid function.[100, 101, 102, 103] Here again are other examples of the overlap of metabolic conditions and poor quality or interrupted sleep. Other recent medical studies have shown a strong association between sleep abnormalities and impairments in thyroid function, especially hypothyroidism or low thyroid function.[104]

Compounding this seemingly endless list of links between metabolic stress, poor quality sleep, and thyroid function is the fact that hypothyroid disease (low thyroid function) is known to be a risk for cardiovascular disease, obesity, osteoporosis, Alzheimer's disease, and memory loss in the aging. All of these interlinked conditions and diseases are related to the metabolic syndrome, which again is intimately related to metabolic stress occurring during the nighttime.

One therapeutic intervention might impact all of these conditions and diseases. It is the simple strategy of restocking the liver glycogen store with honey before bedtime and again in the morning, thus reducing or eliminating metabolic stress altogether. Confirmatory clinical evidence will have to await more investigation, but there is no downside to getting a head start on prevention.

Honey for Depression

Depression is a multi-factored, complex family of conditions that affect various brain regions in different ways. The causes of clinical depression include factors from three broad categories of stress experienced by all of us: psychological, physiological and environmental. The focus in this book has been on the physiologic or metabolic stress as opposed to the psychological or environmental. However, stress from whatever the cause is universally associated with elevations in glucocorticoid (cortisol) release. The link between elevated cortisol levels and anxiety and depression has been established in several studies.[105, 106, 107] In advance of actual clinical manifestation of depression, poor quality and shortened sleep have been shown to be causative factors. Environmental and psychological stresses are also contributors, many of which are difficult to control.

The interrelationship between physiological and psychological stress is also evidenced in several ways. Depression is known to be associated with defects in the central nervous system's cortisol receptors. This results in reactivation of the negative feedback signals required to reduce cortisol levels. Pharmacological agents used in the treatment of depression known as tricyclic anti-depressants and selective serotonin re-uptake inhibitors (SSRIs) reverse this stress-induced deficiency of serotonin in the space between nerve cells, in effect increasing the level of neurotransmitters present. In a paper published in 1998, these findings were confirmed and this connection between depression and chronic elevation of cortisol or cortisol-driven metabolic stress was again demonstrated.[108]

Another excellent example of the interrelated dynamics that occur in depression comes from patients who suffer from Cushing's syndrome, a disease that results from chronic overproduction of cortisol. These individuals are at high risk of depression.[109] However, when the cortisol levels are returned to normal, the depression is relieved.

There are also powerful links between metabolic stress from elevated cortisol levels, depression and memory processing.[110] It is the hippocampal region of the brain that is affected most directly. The hippocampus plays a significant role in metabolism, in sleep regulation, and in short-term memory and memory consolidation, and it is the region of the brain most at risk from cortisol excess. In other words, it is the hippocampus that is most affected by chronic, recurrent metabolic stress.

The research by Dinan, previously cited, provides additional information regarding the interrelationship between stress physiology, memory, and mental acuity.[111] Earlier it was noted how low levels of liver glycogen result in increased physiologic stress and negatively impact mental acuity.

Fortunately, metabolic stress is controllable, and therein is the greatest hope for those suffering from depression. This form of stress is driven by hunger signals from the brain, or brain hunger. All the modern metabolic diseases, of which depression is one manifestation, can be improved by optimal provision of fuel for the brain at critical times during the 24-hour cycle. The key is the formation and storage of an adequate supply of liver glycogen — the only glycogen store that provides glucose to the circulation for brain uptake during the night and at other times when blood glucose is low.

By simply maintaining liver glycogen stores, one can limit the effects of cortisol activation and thereby improve brain processing, and in turn, have a positive impact on depression by decreasing cortisol levels. It is interesting to note that much research is being done currently with regard to cortisol antagonists as potential treatment for severe depression. It seems that a much easier solution would be to simply take a little honey. Honey forms liver glycogen directly. A stable reserve of liver glycogen eliminates brain hunger, reduces metabolic stress, and lowers the risk of depression without the complicating side-effects of medication.

THE BENEFITS OF HONEY
FOR SLEEP

"Sleep with honey. It's good for your health."

S leep is an energy-driven, physiological process. When we retire to bed, our body goes to work (or should do so). This simple statement of scientific fact contradicts much of modern popular thinking regarding what exactly happens during the eight hours of the night fast. This thinking is based on the notion that because no physical exercise occurs, sleep is a process that somehow uses little or no energy. From this we wrongly conclude that eating before going to bed is not necessary and will result in food being converted into fat and stored as such—a myth passed on from generation to generation. Unfortunately, some medical professionals also believe this myth.[112] Nothing could be further from the scientific truth.

Most of the energy required for the brain, kidneys, and red blood cells during sleep (about 10 grams per hour) must be obtained from the liver. Quality, healthful, restorative sleep is dependent on an adequate stock of glucose to fuel the brain throughout the night, but the liver can only store about 80 grams of glucose as glycogen. Therefore, to avoid triggering metabolic stress, the liver glycogen store must be "topped off" before going to bed. When fueled by adequate liver glycogen during nighttime, restorative sleep promotes recovery physiology, and recovery physiology is reparative — a vigorous rebuilding and restorative activity affecting all tissues in the body.

Recovery physiology is also primarily fat-burning physiology, utilizing fat stores for energy requirements. But fat-burning physiology functions at nighttime only when the brain is provided with an adequate glucose supply to get through the night.

Honey is the perfect food to provide energy for the brain during the night fast because it ensures that recovery physiology can continue uninterrupted. The primary reasons for this are simple and straightforward:

- Honey packs a dense caloric load: a small amount provides a relatively large amount of energy.
- Honey presents the gut with a low digestive burden. Absorption into the blood stream is rapid, leaving the GI tract quiet for the night.
- Honey ingestion results in immediate formation of liver glycogen, toping off the brain fuel reserve, thus ensuring that the brain will be well fueled during the night.

A well-fueled brain is a contented brain. Because sleep is a high-energy enterprise for the brain, it is essential that the brain be provided with enough glucose for fuel to last throughout the eight hours of the night fast. *Fueling the liver with honey before bedtime does just that.* At all times, but especially during sleep, the brain actively and aggressively defends its energy supply when glucose is scarce. When glucose from the liver glycogen reserve runs low, as in the early morning hours, the brain activates metabolic stress to ensure its own energy supply.

Chronic and repeated disruption of sleep by metabolic stress eventually results in impaired glucose regulation and increased insulin resistance. Chronic repeated activation of metabolic stress ultimately results in one or more conditions or diseases grouped together in the metabolic syndrome. Poor-quality sleep or shortened sleep secondary to metabolic stress when experienced cumulatively over weeks, months or years equates with sleep depravation.

Sleep depravation (defined as less than six hours of sleep each night) is itself a major risk factor for multiple diseases. Multiple epidemiologic studies have shown that sleep depravation is associated with the following: [113]

- An increase in obesity due to an increase in the production of ghrelin, the primary hunger hormone
- An increased incidence of insulin resistance and diabetes
- An increase in the rate of strokes by a factor of four
- Accelerated memory loss and increased evidence of brain deterioration
- An increased risk of osteoporosis
- An increase risk of heart disease, including a 48% increase in early cardiac-related death and increased mortality from heart disease
- An overall increase in mortality by a factor of four
- An increased risk for colon cancer

The combination of metabolic stress during sleep and cumulative sleep depravation has a profound negative impact on health. Sleep without stress is conducive for recovery and restoration of body organs, tissues, and immune system functions. Honey ingestion before bedtime reduces or eliminates metabolic stress during the nighttime, improves sleep quality, and increases the duration of sleep, and thus reduces the risks for these diseases. The fact that honey promotes restorative sleep makes honey a powerful *revolutionary* food in preventing disease and restoring health.

The simple strategy of consuming a tablespoon or two of honey before bedtime will provide an adequate supply of fuel reserve for the brain throughout the nighttime and ensure that sleep is restful and uninterrupted by metabolic stress.

Honey for Sleep Disorders

Obstructive sleep apnea (OSA), or sleep apnea, is a condition of interrupted breathing during sleep that reduces oxygen delivery to the brain and creates a "reflex" arousal and interruption of sleep. The cycle often continues throughout the night, resulting in significant sleep loss, fatigue, and excessive daytime sleepiness the following day.

Sleep apnea increases the risk for all the diseases known collectively as the metabolic syndrome: heart disease, diabetes, and obesity. The increased risk is the result of chronic increased metabolic stress and inflammation every night. Sleep apnea is emerging as a consistent common link among other diseases and conditions caused by poor-quality sleep and chronic overnight stress – a list that includes depression and Alzheimer's disease.

The easiest and most direct way to reduce this overnight stress and reduce the risks of all of these conditions is to provide the brain with a sufficient fuel supply from the liver during nighttime. The best way to do this is by the ingestion of 1 or 2 tablespoons of quality, unfiltered honey to initiate restorative sleep and promote recovery physiology. Additionally, the production and release of adrenal stress hormones is reduced, allowing sleep to continue uninterrupted throughout the night.

It is not to be inferred that honey will cure sleep apnea. However, the reduction of metabolic stress during sleep does reduce the risks, not only of sleep apnea, but also of other associated conditions and diseases.

A New "Believer's" Story

(As told by Dr. Fessenden in *The Honey Revolution–Abridged*)

As a woman stepped to the microphone following a recent presentation on "The Effects of Honey on Human Metabolism" at a beekeepers convention in Saskatchewan, I wondered briefly what might be coming from this somewhat overweight individual.

She began by saying, "I have joined the honey revolution!" In surprised and curious silence, I waited for her to continue. "Six months ago I was very much overweight, much more so than now. I had borderline diabetes, and my doctor was considering what interventions might be necessary for my elevated blood sugar and cholesterol. I couldn't sleep more than 3 or 4 hours a night without waking up hungry. Sometimes it took me an hour to get back to sleep. I had purchased your book **The Honey Revolution** a year ago, and I decided that it was time to see if your advice would work."

She paused briefly and started again, "I am happy to report that I have lost a lot of weight, and my blood sugar and cholesterol levels are normal. My doctor was happy and I was thrilled, but more importantly . . . "

What could be better than what she had already reported? Then she continued, "I sleep through the night without interruption. I wake up feeling rested. I haven't felt this good in my life! Thank you for your book, and thank God for honey!"

Honey and Dreams

Dreams are known to occur primarily during the portion of sleep known as rapid eye movement (REM) sleep. Newborns may spend up to 80% of their sleep cycle in REM sleep. Adults above the age of 60 typically have only 60 minutes of REM sleep and that amount decreases even further as one ages. REM sleep is important for many aspects of human development and physiology including memory consolidation and learning,[114, 115, 116, 117] and proper central nervous system development in both children and adults.[118, 119] Reduction or elimination of REM sleep is associated with several mild psychological disturbances including anxiety, irritability, hallucinations, and difficulty concentrating.[120]

The most common and interesting anecdotes reported from those who consume a tablespoon or two of honey before bedtime relate to an increase in dreams during sleep and dream recall. Dreams are more vivid, intense, and dream recall is profound. The reports have become so frequent that conclusive opinions are merited.

The ingestion of honey before bedtime provides sufficient fuel for the brain so that REM sleep occurs in its normal cycles, uninterrupted by metabolic stress. Honey also reduces metabolic and oxidative stress, both of which affect the duration and quality of sleep. Logic would support the fact that liver glycogen replenishment prior to bedtime ensures restorative sleep and increases REM sleep, both of which are known to facilitate offline processing, memory consolidation, and learning.

This hypothesis presents us, therefore, with a model for improved learning and memory consolidation. More research is needed to confirm this. However, in the meantime, *there is no risk associated with consuming honey before bedtime*. Those who have begun this habit may find themselves well ahead of the game in experiencing improved brain function.

Honey, Melatonin and the Brain

Melatonin is a hormone with a wide range of beneficial functions. Research over the last two decades suggests that melatonin is critical in memory and learning. Its role in memory consolidation and learning in cerebral metabolism is critical. Some researchers now regard melatonin as the *learning hormone*.

In addition, melatonin is a potent antioxidant; it reduces stress by inhibiting cortisol and adrenaline release; it exhibits anti-aging potential; it promotes quality sleep and recovery physiology; it exhibits neuro-protective and anti-carcinogenic properties; and it relieves anxiety.

Given the fact that quality sleep is critical to memory consolidation and human learning, it would seem logical to conclude that optimizing recovery physiology by reducing chronic overproduction of adrenal stress hormones (which inhibit melatonin) and maximizing the production and release of melatonin would be a sound investment in promoting the health of the brain. The only practical way that this may be achieved is by optimally replenishing liver glycogen stores in the period before sleep. And the gold standard food for this purpose is pure, unfiltered honey. This strategy produces the exact metabolic environment required to allow for the release of melatonin, growth hormone, and IGF-1 — the key hormones of memory consolidation and learning.

Honey for Memory and Learning

One of the more exciting benefits of consuming honey relates to its potential role in aiding or enhancing memory consolidation and learning. Many investigations over the past ten years have demonstrated the effects of hormones, specifically cortisol, on the hippocampus, a part of the brain belonging to the limbic system and responsible for memory and spatial navigation.[121, 122, 123, 124] The hippocampus has many receptors for cortisol, and when cortisol attaches to these receptors, memory and learning are negatively affected.

We are not suggesting that one can get smarter by eating honey. What we are suggesting is that regular consumption of honey will help to prevent or eliminate the effects of elevated levels of cortisol on that part of the brain responsible for memory consolidation and learning. When cortisol levels are reduced, the hippocampus functions normally and memory and learning are improved.

Additional animal and human studies have shown that metabolic stress from excessive cortisol levels is responsible for memory impairment, caused by brain nerve cell excitability and eventual cell loss. These results are consistent across a variety of conditions that result in excessive glucocorticoid (cortisol) levels. For example, patients with Cushing's syndrome who are taking therapeutic doses of steroids[125, 126] have been observed to have spatial memory deficits, deficits in verbal recall, and increases in anxiety. In a lengthy review that focused on the hormonal changes associated with pregnancy, the patterns of memory loss both during and after pregnancy indicated the cause as being hippocampal dysfunction. Pregnancy is known to be associated with elevated levels of cortisol.[127] These same deficits have also been observed in animals given excessive doses of synthetic glucocorticoids. Memory performance improved with reduction in the excess cortisol levels for both volunteers and patients with Cushing's syndrome.[128, 129]

Regular daily consumption of honey has a direct effect on the levels of cortisol produced in the body. When the liver glycogen reserves remain adequate for brain function, circulating cortisol levels remain lower. Cortisol is not released in an attempt to ensure backup fuel for the brain. It really is that simple. Regular honey consumption prevents the chronic and excessive release of cortisol, which is the principle cause of metabolic stress. Chronic metabolic stress impacts memory by damaging hippocampal neurons.

In one rather elegant, yet simple animal study,[130] rats fed honey over a twelve-month period were observed to have better spatial memory and reduced anxiety as compared to those fed a sucrose diet. The authors speculated that as different areas of the hippocampus mediate these behaviors and these areas are susceptible to oxidative damage over time, honey might have been responsible for the positive results because of its antioxidant content. I would add that honey also reduces intracellular inflammation and reduces or eliminates the effects of insulin resistance, allowing brain cells to function properly. As regular honey consumption has an effect on preventing excess cortisol release, it seems perfectly reasonable to state therefore, that honey can prevent memory degradation and lessen anxiety by its role in limiting cortisol production and release, by providing antioxidants necessary to reverse oxidative damage, and by improving intracellular energy utilization.

Honey for Mental Acuity, Impaired Cognition and Dementia

It is one thing to observe improvements or changes in memory function in laboratory animals given dietary changes (honey versus sucrose) over some extended period of time as in the study referenced above. Consider also the experience common to many of us of a transient dip in mental alertness or acuity in the early to mid-afternoon consistent with falling blood glucose as a result of insulin release in the post-lunch period. A third observation associates diabetes with cognitive impairment or decline in cognitive ability such as seen in dementias, Alzheimer's disease, and other neuro-degenerative conditions. What about the observations that link poor classroom performance and lack of attentiveness with missing a good breakfast? Or the repeated cycles of a quick sugar "fix" followed by a lethargic phase experienced in young people who consume canned sodas throughout the day.

Is there a metabolic phenomenon or causative thread that ties all of these observations together? Medical research is beginning to connect the dots.[131] Episodes of hypoglycemia (low blood sugar) have a profound effect on the hippocampus portion of the brain in both patients with and without diabetes. Long-term effects of severe hypoglycemia include significant risks of cognitive impairment.

In diabetic patients, these risks are more severe, simply because episodes of hypoglycemia are more frequent. Impaired glucose metabolism, and insulin resistance have also been associated with poor cognitive performance, increased risk of cognitive impairment and dementia. Other studies link the metabolic syndrome to dementia and Alzheimer's disease.[132] It is believed that oxidative damage to the hippocampus due to repeated moderate episodes of hypoglycemia (and the resultant elevated cortisol levels) is the common damaging thread among all of these conditions.[133]

Many recent investigations seem to agree on the fact that both repeated episodes of hypoglycemia and chronically elevated blood sugar levels have the same long-term effect on the brain.[134, 135, 136] The stabilization and regulation of blood sugar, therefore, seems to be a simple therapeutic solution leading to improved brain function and the elimination of memory loss and dementia. How better to accomplish this than by the regular consumption of honey. Honey, by virtue of its rapid absorption and formation of liver glycogen, which fuels the brain, provides the ideal safeguard.

Elizabeth's Story

(Adapted from *Feed Your Brain First*.)

E lizabeth was in her early 60s when her husband began noticing changes. Car keys would disappear. The burner on the stove would be left on after meal preparation was complete. Words would be missed in casual conversation – everyday words with well-known meanings seemed to be forgotten. Her dress habits, which had always been proper, even immaculate, seemed to slip occasionally – the same outfit two days in a row or jewelry that didn't quite match or confusion about what went with what. At times, she just appeared "lost" or lonely and withdrawn.

It all happened so subtly without fanfare or warning. It "just wasn't like her" was the way her husband described her mental state to her physician. Physical examination and multiple diagnostic tests revealed that Elizabeth was experiencing the early onset of Alzheimer's disease (AD). Except for having adult-onset diabetes for several years, Elizabeth was, by her family's admission, in fairly good health. She had no history of high blood pressure or strokes or heart irregularities. Her memory, until recent months, had been exceptional. Everyone who knew her considered her bright and outgoing. No one in her family had experienced anything like this, no dementia, no strokes, and no premature memory loss.

"How could this be happening?" her husband questioned. Their lives were happy and uncomplicated. Their interests centered on family, which lived close by, and several grandchildren whom Elizabeth doted on with regularity. Now, even the youngest wondered at times if Grandma was all right.

Virtually unheard of before the 1960s, Alzheimer's disease now touches nearly one in five extended families and by 2050 is projected to affect one in 85 individuals worldwide. Its increase in incidence has been attributed to many factors, though no specific causative factors have been isolated. Individuals with hypertension, increased cholesterol, diabetes, and a history of smoking seem to have a higher risk for developing AD.

For Elizabeth and her family, the thought of experiencing a tortuous march toward certain mental deterioration with little hope for treatment seemed devastating. What clues exist that might lead to an understanding of Elizabeth's plight? The discoveries of medical science over the past 40 years give us few to consider. But by connecting the dots linking Elizabeth's metabolic history, some general insights are possible.

The chronic elevation in blood sugar (hyperglycemia) that characterized Elizabeth's diabetes produced a chronic elevation in insulin release (hyperinsulinemia) that eventually resulted in insulin resistance, a condition where the insulin that is produced is not effective. From the brain's perspective, this deprives the individual brain cells (neurons) of needed energy by a process known as increased intracellular oxidative stress. Over time, the brain cells ability to generate ATP (the energy source within the mitochondria of each neuron) is decreased or compromised. When the mitochondria fail, glucose cannot be absorbed into the glial cells of the brain, those cells responsible for delivering the fuel supply to each neuron. Without energy, brain cells cannot function properly and eventually die.

At the same time, another sinister action takes place within the synapses (the interspaces between neurons) of the brain. Glutamate, the primary brain signal neuro-transmitter, accumulates within the synapses due to the failure of the mitochondria to generate ATP properly. This accumulation of glutamate is toxic to brain tissue, further compromising brain function and resulting in chronic levels of cortisol to be released from the adrenal glands.

Finally, increased cortisol levels have a profoundly negative effect on the hippocampus, the portion of the brain most responsible for memory consolidation, short-term memory and learning, contributing to the loss of recent memory.

While one cannot be entirely certain that this catastrophic chain of events was responsible for Elizabeth's AD, the logic points in that direction. Over the years, she consumed more and more carbohydrates, partly in an attempt to "eat healthy" by cutting down on fat. Decades of high carbohydrate consumption (especially simple sugars) resulted in chronically elevated blood sugar levels that led to insulin resistance, diabetes and ultimately to the loss of brain function that resulted in her early symptoms of AD.

Honey and Alzheimer's Disease

The seriousness of Alzheimer's disease (AD) and its impact on Americans and their families is best illustrated by these facts and figures from the Alzheimer's Association 2013:

- Alzheimer's disease is the sixth leading cause of death in the United States.
- An estimated 5.2 million Americans of all ages have AD and that number is expected to increase by 40% to 7.1 million by 2025 and to 13.8 million by 2050.
- One in three seniors die with AD or another form of dementia.
- In 2013, the direct costs of caring for those with AD will total an estimated $203 billion.[137]

The link between impaired glucose metabolism, the metabolic syndrome, and abnormal sleep patterns has been previously discussed. Growing evidence also supports the link between diabetes and AD.[138] This link supports the concept that AD is fundamentally a metabolic disease with molecular and biochemical features that correspond with diabetes mellitus and insulin resistance.[139] The situation is complicated, however, by the fact that AD may arise in association with systemic insulin resistance diseases, including diabetes, obesity, and non-alcoholic fatty liver disease or as a separate disease. AD is also being associated with interrupted sleep, poor quality sleep and sleep apnea.[140, 141]

It is apparent that all of the metabolic conditions discussed so far have strong inter-connections and associated risk factors. In addition, clinical and experimental studies in humans and animals have shown marked immune system impairments when sleep loss is experienced.[142] These connections would suggest that an improvement in sleep patterns in the elderly might significantly lessen the manifestation and progression of all of the diseases related to the metabolic syndrome, including AD.

The recommendation that a dose of honey before bedtime should be one essential aspect of treatment bears serious consideration. Honey allows recovery physiology to occur without interruption during rest. Honey reduces the level of cortisol produced secondary to brain starvation. Cortisol negatively affects the hippocampus, the center for short-term memory and memory consolidation. It is reasonable to conclude that reducing or eliminating potential damage to the hippocampus from excessive cortisol levels would therefore improve memory consolidation and retrieval. The fact that honey also stabilizes blood sugar and reduces the risk of insulin resistance and diabetes, which are known to be causative factors in AD, further suggests that honey might play a role in the reduction in the prevalence of AD.

Honey for Hypertension

The inclusion of this section on honey and its potential effect on high blood pressure in the section on sleep, rather than in the section on cardiovascular disease, is intentional. The association between sleep depravation or poor quality sleep and elevated blood pressure has been known for some time. Individuals that are deprived of sleep have acutely increased blood pressure, which goes along with increased sympathetic nervous system activity. It is thought that repeated and prolonged sleep depravation over several weeks or months could lead to chronic hypertension due to sustained elevations in blood pressure and heart rate and elevated sympathetic nervous system activity. Professor James Gangswisch and his associates from the School of Public Health at Columbia University in New York published an article in 2006 that found that interrupted or short sleep could be a risk factor for hypertension.[143] In theory then, if you could find an easy drug free way to prolong sleep and improve sleep quality, you could easily reduce your risk for hypertension. If you could also reduce the metabolic stress brought on during rest when the brain runs low on fuel, you would reduce catecholamine production that raises blood pressure and heart rate.

Honey does that. Consuming honey before bedtime, which ensures an adequate glycogen reserve in the liver, results in longer, less interrupted sleep. When its fuel reserve is secure, the brain does not need to go in search of additional fuel in the early morning hours. Consuming honey before bedtime thus reduces the release of adrenalin, a catecholamine that raises blood pressure and heart rate.

Though it cannot be stated categorically that eating honey will reduce your blood pressure, suggesting honey for hypertension serves as another example of "connecting the dots" in which normal physiology is linked to a predicted outcome of some intervention. Honey promotes restorative sleep, which is defined as improved quality and longer duration sleep. Longer sleep means a reduced risk for hypertension. A reduced risk for hypertension within a population means fewer individuals needing treatment for that widespread condition. The consumption of honey would seem to be a very efficient and cost effective strategy for reducing the risks of hypertension by simply consuming a natural food that contains no risk.

THE EFFECTS OF HONEY ON THE IMMUNE SYSTEM

O ptimum functioning of the immune system is profoundly interconnected with other aspects of metabolic function within the body. Many clinical studies have demonstrated the association between sleep loss and compromised immune function. The provision of an adequate and sustained energy supply for the brain during the period of nighttime fasting promotes restorative sleep and improved immune system functioning, and the ingestion of honey before bedtime makes this possible.

One of the more amazing evidences of honey's potential role in immune system enhancement comes from a study involving the use of a special type of honey (known as LifeMel Honey or LMH) in the treatment of cancer patients.[144] Dr. Jamal Zidon and his associates described these results from a study conducted at several hospitals in Israel on severely ill cancer patients with multiple types of cancers. These patients all suffered from acute febrile neutropenia (AFN), a life-threatening condition in which the white blood cell count is dangerously low. All of the patients required treatment with Colony Stimulating Factor (CSF), an expensive drug given to boost the immune system response.

The patients, all being treated with various chemotherapy protocols, were also given a *teaspoon* of LMH for five days before their second round of chemotherapy doses. Remarkably, there was no recurrence of neutropenia after the honey treatment. Forty percent of the patients had no need for additional CSF treatments. Most patients included in the study group showed increased neutrophil counts, decreased occurrences of thrombocytopenia (low platelet count), and stabilized hemoglobin levels. No specific biochemical mechanisms were given to explain the results, however the findings were consistent with other published reports citing the immune system enhancement effects of honey.

Clinical and laboratory studies have demonstrated that regular consumption of honey results in elevation of platelet counts, stabilization of hemoglobin levels, and improvements in white blood cell counts, all results that are associated with improved immune system functioning.[145, 146]

Honey and Allergies

Perhaps the most frequently asked question pertaining to the healthful benefits of consuming honey is "Will eating *local honey* help my allergies?" For decades, it has been a belief of many that exposure to small doses of pollen contained in honey will help desensitize one to particular allergens and reduce allergic symptoms. Where better to find small doses of pollens than in honey produced from the local region where one lives.

There are a couple of challenges to this belief that need to be considered. First of all, this is probably one of the most researched aspects of potential health benefits from honey reported in the scientific literature. The results have been rather non-conclusive for a number of reasons, including the number of confounding variables associated with the allergic phenomenon, the lack of adequate control groups, and the complexity of the body's immune responses. The FDA does not allow pollen marketers in the United States to make health claims about their product because no scientific basis for these claims has ever been proven. However much anecdotal evidence continues to support the theory that eating *local* honey will help reduce one's allergic responses.

The second issue relates to the nature of pollens to which humans are allergic. Most pollen found in honey is the type known as entomophilous, which is pollen dispersed by animals or insects. This pollen is heavier and stickier and does not typically become airborne. Most flowering plants and trees frequented by honeybees produce this type of pollen, which is usually not associated with allergic reactions in humans. Generally pollens that cause allergies in humans are those of anemophilous plants, which produce light, dry pollen that is dispersed by air currents over a wide region. Such plants produce large quantities of this lightweight pollen, which when airborne can be easily inhaled and come into contact with the sensitive mucous membranes in the nose resulting in typical allergic reactions.

Given the fact that the pollen most likely found in *local honey* is not pollen to which humans are allergic, it is unlikely that consuming local honey will desensitize you to these pollens. However, *that is not to say the honey will not help allergies.* The immune system enhancements brought about by consuming honey are profound and generalized. The allergic response in humans is mediated by a healthy immune system. Therefore, it is reasonable to assume that honey will positively affect your immune system in dealing with local allergens, even though there is no scientific proof that honey will help by way of desensitizing you to those same allergens. This is one of those areas in which eating honey will do no harm, and might even have a therapeutic benefit–just not in the way most folks believe.

Honey and Cancer

Cancer is diagnosed over 30,000 times *every day* in individuals around the world and *every day* over 20,000 people die from various forms of the disease.[147] The standard treatments for cancer are surgery, radiotherapy, and chemotherapy, each beset with serious side effects. Radiation and chemotherapy are themselves toxic to other viable cells in the body. Many natural products have been studied for their potential preventative and treatment capabilities. Within the past few years, honey has been extensively researched in this regard, with very surprising and encouraging results.

There are still many unanswered questions, such as, why sugar is carcinogenic, yet honey, which is basically sugar, has many anti-carcinogenic properties. Much more research is needed to confirm the preliminary information gained from cell cultures and animal experimentation and the application of these studies to humans. Prospective randomized controlled clinical trials are needed to validate the usefulness of honey alone or as adjuvant therapy. Yet the encouraging news is that honey seems to exhibit seven or eight non-invasive, non-toxic mechanisms of action that offer hope for cancer patients.

This section on honey and cancer might just as well have been included in the section on the metabolic benefits of consuming honey as many of honey's benefits relate to its antioxidant and anti-inflammatory activity. However, because honey is a potent stimulant for the immune system in humans, it is included here.

It is not to be inferred from this section that consuming honey might cure a person with cancer. However, we are suggesting that honey, when consumed regularly may play a role in cancer prevention, and in an evolving therapeutic role as more of honey's anti-carcinogenic activities are discovered and confirmed, something that cannot be said about all other refined sugars and artificial sweeteners.

We do know that the consumption of *honey directly stimulates the production of immune system factors* by virtue of both direct and indirect mechanisms. Honey stimulates the production of antibodies, lymphocytes, monocytes, eosinophils and natural cancer killer cells, thus enhancing the immunologic response to cancer.[148, 149, 150, 151] Honey also acts indirectly by inhibiting metabolic stress, reducing the production of cortisol. Cortisol is one of the most powerful hormone inhibitors of immune function. Thus honey is immunoprotective by its action in reducing cortisol levels.

Honey exhibits powerful anti-inflammatory activities, some of which have been documented earlier. Chronic inflammation is linked to cancer formation. Phenolic compounds (or natural phenols) in honey are responsible for its anti-inflammatory activity.[152]

In the cancer cell, the mitochondria, the intracellular power plants or energy producers, malfunction. However, the clever cancer cell hyper-activates or accelerates the first stage of glucose metabolism that occurs within the mitochondria, producing pyruvate. Pyruvate is then converted to lactic acid, which is then metabolized as fuel. This process is less efficient than normal glucose metabolism and uses up huge quantities of glucose with less energy production. The result is that lean body tissue (protein) must now be degraded to create new glucose and feed the cancer. This is part of the reason for the rapid and progressive weight loss experienced by many cancer patients with many types of cancers.

Under normal conditions, a cell undergoing abnormal formation or mutation would destroy itself, a sort of programmed cell death or apoptosis as it is called, thus protecting the rest of the body from a metastasizing mutation. However, cancer interrupts this process by causing the mitochondria to malfunction. The diseased cells cannot destroy themselves. *Honey consumption reactivates the mitochondria*, which then induces apoptosis in these affected cells by several various methods, allowing the affected cells to die.[153, 154, 155]

Honey also inhibits the mutagenic (cellular mutation) ability of cancer cells to replicate.[156, 157] Honey has also been shown to arrest or suppress tumor cell proliferation in multiple types of cancers types including colon cancer, gliomas and melanoma cancers.[158, 159, 160]

There are many bioactive compounds in honey that improve glucose metabolism and storage and improve insulin signaling. These include trace amounts of vitamins, minerals, amino acids, bioflavonoids, organic acids, nitric oxide, and other volatiles. Medicine has only just begun to appreciate all of the reasons why the consumption of honey, as compared to other refined sugars, HFCS or artificial sweeteners, which have none of these properties, might reduce risk of some forms of cancer and prove to be therapeutic in others.

Consumption of refined sugars and HFCS results in the release of excessive amounts of insulin and eventually leads to insulin resistance and increased risk of cancers due to impaired mitochondrial function described above. *Honey reduces the amount of insulin release necessary* due to its balanced fructose/glucose content and its improved insulin signaling. Honey acts as "proto-insulin" which in effect reduces the requirement for insulin and improves glucose metabolism. This fact alone may prove to be one of the great unsung, key secrets of honey, a wonderful energy boosting food that improves insulin-signaling activity without the benefit of added insulin production. On the surface this appears to be a contradiction. This observation has potent implications for human nutrition.

The powerful health message is that consumption of honey might reduce the risks of cancer by reducing metabolic stress and improving glucose metabolism. The evidence is growing. The simple message is clear and compelling.

In summary, the following are the primary anti-cancer benefits of consuming honey:

- Honey stimulates the production of antibodies, lymphocytes, monocytes, and other natural cancer killer cells.
- Honey inhibits the production of cortisol, a powerful immune system inhibitor.
- Honey reactivates the mitochondria, allowing them to function properly.
- Honey inhibits mutagenic ability of cancer cells.

THE ANTIMICROBIAL BENEFITS OF HONEY

"The slight regard at this time paid to the medicinal virtues of Honey, is an instance of neglect men shew to common objects, whatever their value: acting in contempt, as it were, of the immediate hand of providence, which has in general made those things most frequent, which have the greatest uses; and for that reason, we seek from the remotest part of the world, medicines of harsh and violent operation for our relief in several disorders, under which we should never suffer, if we would use what the Bee collects for us at our doors." (John Hill, MD, 1759)[161]

The use of honey as a topical treatment for wounds, burns, and infections has been documented in recorded history dating back to before 2000 BC in Egyptian writings. Twenty-first century science has confirmed what the ancients believed and what men throughout the centuries have known experientially and intuitively. Honey is therapeutic. When applied as a topical antibiotic, honey's healing properties cover a wide range of infective agents. Researchers from New Zealand and Australia have led the way in the study of honey and its antibiotic potential for decades. Perhaps best of all, the use of honey in this manner comes without side effects.

In 2002, Joe Traynor published a wonderful treatise entitled ***Honey The Gourmet Medicine.***"[162] In his book, Traynor documents that the effectiveness of honey in destroying bacteria comes from at least four properties found in various honey varietals. However, all four properties are not found in all honey varietals to the same degree.

The Four Anti-microbial Properties of Honey
First of all honey is hyperosmolar – that is, its water content is very low, generally between 18 and 20% or lower. When in contact with other tissues, honey literally absorbs water from cells, killing them.

Second, honey is very acidic. The pH of honey averaged across many varietals is less than 4.0 making it more acidic than most foods and even some acids. Low acidity inhibits the growth of most bacteria.

Third, honey has the ability to generate hydrogen peroxide under certain conditions. Hydrogen peroxide has been used as a disinfectant for decades, but because it is unstable in the presence of light and air, it is difficult to store and utilize. Hydrogen peroxide in high concentrations is also quite toxic to human tissue making it less attractive as a topical disinfectant. Honey solves this dilemma and provides an ideal mechanism for producing hydrogen peroxide in controlled amounts.

Honey contains the enzyme glucose oxidase. This enzyme comes from the honeybee, and small amounts of it remain in honey as it is extracted, processed and packaged for sale. Glucose oxidase works on the glucose in honey, breaking it down into gluconic acid and hydrogen peroxide. However, the enzyme is not active in pure honey because of its low pH and low sodium content. Activation of glucose oxidase requires a pH of at least 5.5 and a sodium content of at least 2,300 parts per million (ppm). The sodium content of pure honey is only 20 to 40 ppm.

Honey when applied to a burn, wound or infected tissue begins to work its wonders only as serum from the tissues dilutes the honey, raising its pH, and adds sodium, thus activating glucose oxidase. The action of glucose oxidase delivers small controlled portions of hydrogen peroxide directly to the site of an infection where the honey is applied. Thus, the miracle of pure honey is its hydrogen peroxide generating *potential*. Traynor summarizes this capability of honey with these words:

> *"Thus, minute doses of hydrogen peroxide are continually released from the honey, directly to where they are most needed. Could man devise a more perfect, slow-release antimicrobial product for treating wounds? If a billion dollar, biomedical company gave their research and development scientists unlimited time and resources, it is doubtful they could equal what nature has already provided in honey. It's enough to make even the most skeptical scientist believe in a higher being, as if God, in His wisdom, provided man with a perfect elixir to treat wounds and infections. Doctors in the U.S., with rare exceptions, have rejected this gift."*[163]

This potential ability to produce hydrogen peroxide is not found in all honey. Some honey even contains small quantities of the enzyme catalase. Catalase neutralizes hydrogen peroxide, thus diminishing the effectiveness of honey as an antimicrobial.

Fourth, honey contains other floral factors obtained from nectar. One recently discovered ingredient in honey is methylglyoxal (MGO). MGO is perhaps related to what Peter Molan from New Zealand has called the Unique Manuka Factor or UMF found in higher concentrations in Manuka honey made from the flowers of the Manuka bush in New Zealand (also known as the leptospermum bush in Australia).

In January of 2008, Professor Thomas Henle, head of the Institute of Food Chemistry at the Technical University of Dresden, published an article in which he refers to the results of a study that "unambiguously demonstrates for the first time that methylglyoxal is directly responsible for the antibacterial activity of Manuka Honey."[164] Researchers at the university analyzed 40 samples of honey from various sources around the world, including New Zealand honeys. They found MGO levels in Manuka honeys were up to 1,000 times higher than non-Manuka honeys. This observation is critical as MGO is highly toxic to the cells of the body, a fact discussed earlier in the section on Honey for Diabetes.

Other constituents and properties of honey have been identified more recently that confirm its powerful antimicrobial properties and mechanisms of action.[165] These include the presence in honey of antioxidants, polyphenols, flavonoids, enzymes and peptides, as well as honey's ability to positively affect the immune system and provide anti-inflammatory actions.

The important fact to note is that all honey, regardless of the varietal, possesses some of the properties that make honey effective against bacteria. Multiple varietals of honey were tested by Dr. Shona Blair and her associates from the University of Sydney in Australia. There was wide variation among these varietals as to their effectiveness as an antimicrobial. Among the honey varietals used in their study, the effective mean concentrations of honey necessary to kill or inhibit the growth of bacteria varied from just 2 to 16% when applied against more than 60 problematic pathogens studied.[166] These pathogens included several antibiotic resistant micro-organisms, many species of anaerobic bacteria, Candida and Tinea fungi, and biofilms. Sugar solutions used as controls in this study required mean concentrations of greater than 20 to 45% to achieve the same *in vitro* antibacterial effects.

More recent work by Dr. Blair and her team have confirmed both the antibiotic and anti-fungal properties of other honey varietals, though the floral source was not found to be a reliable predictor of the antimicrobial activity of honey.[167] Heat processing was also found to be detrimental to this activity. Despite a large amount of data confirming the antimicrobial activity of honey, there are no studies that support the systemic (or intravenous) use of honey as an antibacterial agent.[168]

Honey and Wound Care

In addition to its antimicrobial properties, honey's effects on wound healing have been widely studied. The world's scientific literature contains hundreds of articles that validate the therapeutic use of honey for skin infections, wounds, burns, traumatic amputations, and ulcers. Unfortunately, the "slight regard . . . paid to the medicinal virtues of Honey" written of by Dr. Hill in 1759 continues in many areas today, especially in the United States. Perhaps, one of the reasons for this was captured by Joe Traynor when he describes honey as "a medicine without a profit."[169]

The data from these studies shows that the wound healing properties of honey include stimulation of tissue growth, enhanced epithelialization (or re-growth of superficial skin), and minimized scar formation.[170] Honey was also found to lower prostaglandin levels (hormones responsible for inflammation) and raise nitric oxide, which might explain the physiologic and therapeutic properties of honey as an agent in wound healing.

Honey has also been found to inhibit biofilm growth.[171] Biofilms and their persistence within wounds are factors contributing to impaired wound healing. Biofilms are microorganisms that secrete a slimy protective coating that makes them resistant to antibiotics. The use of honey on wounds kills these bacteria and limits biofilm formation.

Many personal anecdotal reports also confirm the therapeutic beneficial effects of using honey on wounds. For example, honey when placed on a wound bandage prevents unnecessary wound drying, softens scab formation, and makes removal of bandages much easier and less painful.

Honey for Oral Health, Gingivitis, and Periodontal Disease

Several investigators have looked at the benefits of honey on oral health within the past few years.[172, 173, 174, 175] All of the studies reviewed indicated that honey seems to have a positive therapeutic benefit on dental plaque, gingivitis, and periodontal disease. Honey's primary mechanism of action in providing these benefits is its antibacterial activity. One side benefit of using honey regularly is that as the oral bacterial content is reduced, bad breath caused by these bacteria will be reduced or eliminated.

Honey can be used in the prevention and treatment of oral diseases in the form of mouthwashes, or in specially prepared gum or gel, or by simply ingesting honey directly. One caution needs to be stated, however. Honey is very acidic. Prolonged contact of honey with tooth enamel will begin to damage the enamel. Therefore, it is recommended that if honey is consumed as a natural product, contact with tooth enamel should be minimized. Rinsing the mouth well with water after honey consumption is sufficient to dilute the honey and eliminate the risk of damage to the tooth enamel.

THE MISCELLANEOUS BENEFITS OF CONSUMING HONEY

This final section details a few benefits of consuming honey that do not conveniently fit in the metabolic, sleep, immune system or antibiotic sections. The overlap among mechanisms of action within these sections continues here, as is evident in the section "Honey: the Super Fuel for Exercise" which follows and in the section on "Honey and Aging." The positive effects of honey on blood sugar control and on sleep are present in both.

An additional benefit of honey, mentioned previously, relates to the use of honey for upper respiratory infections in children, particularly those that are associated with a cough. The study by Dr. Ian Paul at the University of Pennsylvania Children's Hospital established that honey was significantly more effective in reducing cough symptoms than the leading over-the-counter cough remedy.[176] This positive effect has been confirmed in multiple other studies in kids since that original study was done.

Honey is an amazing healthful food, regardless of how and for what condition one may consume or use it. Perhaps the most astounding statement one can make about honey is that it accomplishes something for almost every organ, tissue, cell, or system in the body without one complication, risk or negative consequence. Pretty amazing indeed!

Honey: The Super Fuel for Exercise

During exercise, energy stores are being rapidly depleted as if in a state of aggressive starvation. If those energy stores are not rapidly replenished, the body must mobilize all resources to maintain the level of physical output while at the same time maintain all essential metabolic activity. In particular, a fuel supply for the brain must be provided.

During exercise, the brain must be fueled exclusively from the liver glycogen store, while contracting muscles may be fueled from both previously stored muscle glycogen and liver glycogen. An early warning fuel detection system warns the brain when the liver glycogen reserve is running low. This results in the release of cortisol that inhibits insulin and prevents it from driving glucose into the active muscle cells, thus keeping more glucose in circulation to fuel the brain.

However, the tradeoff is that less glucose oxidation takes place within muscle cells at a significant reduction in power output. Honey consumption, therefore, which results in the immediate formation of liver glycogen, is a critical factor in maintaining fuel for the brain and the muscles during exercise.

It is not the intention to provide a comprehensive manual on the various types of foods required for any athlete to fuel for any specific exercise. That information is available in a variety of sport manuals, textbooks, popular exercise and sports magazines and other sporting literature. However, it is the goal herein to provide the recreational or professional athlete general guidelines for fueling for exercise during the day. Throughout this discussion, the state of the liver glycogen store at critical periods will be underscored.

The Five Critical Times for Fueling for Exercise

There are five times during a 24-hour day that are critical for proper exercise fueling:

- The first thing on awakening in the morning
- Before exercise
- During exercise
- After exercise, and
- Before recovery sleep

In the early morning hours or upon awakening, the liver glycogen reserve requires attention. Glycogen stores are nearly depleted after eight hours of sleep, assuming you retired with a fully stocked liver. The brain, if it has not begun to do so already, is responding to the signal from the liver and is correctly sensing that its fuel supply is low.

The liver can hold an average of 75 grams of glycogen. In order to "fill up the tank" you must consume a balance of protein and carbohydrates.[177] Most people would be surprised as to how much food it takes to accomplish this. As an example, two eggs, two strips of bacon, one cup of fruit, one cup of orange juice, a slice of wheat toast with a tablespoon of honey, plus a cup of coffee with cream would just about do the trick.[178] A cup of coffee and a pastry or a bowl of cereal with milk just does not come close to filling the tank, and is consistent with starting off on a long road trip with only a couple of gallons of gas in the tank.

If exercising in the morning is part of your routine, it is best to allow at least 90 minutes after breakfast before beginning your routine to allow for digestion and storage of foods. Then about 15 to 30 minutes before exercise, a small fruit snack, some fruit with honey, 8 ounces of fruit juice or a tablespoon of honey is great for topping off the liver glycogen tank. Exercising without fueling in the morning, though frequently done by many, is a good way to ensure that adrenal-driven stress is initiated unnecessarily.

During exercise, fueling is obviously going to be somewhat dependent on the exercise or sport undertaken. Clearly it is possible to fuel during endurance exercise on a bike as you can easily carry fuel with you, but other protocols such as swimming, running, and skiing may present the athlete with challenges. Regardless of the exercise, the key is to fuel to whatever maximum when possible.

With any moderately intense exercise protocol the optimum is to rehydrate up to one liter of fluids per hour and to include in this approximately 60 grams of carbohydrates, preferably 3 tablespoons of honey. In longer endurance protocols energy bars and gels may be used as well as sport drinks, again keeping firmly in mind that fructose is vital, so that glucose uptake into liver is optimized.

During exercise, contracting muscles extract glucose from the circulation with great efficiency. This may seem contradictory because insulin is inhibited by cortisol released during exercise, and muscle cells normally require insulin signaling to accomplish this glucose uptake. However, contracting muscles extract glucose from the circulation by another method independent of insulin known as *exercise induced muscle uptake of glucose*.[179] As each muscle cell contracts, the glucose transporters are driven to the cell wall allowing for rapid glucose uptake – a process normally requiring insulin. This system, independent of and complementary to insulin, remains in place for up to 48 hours in the post-exercise period, thus ensuring good muscle glycogen replenishment. Muscle cells will extract up to 90% of available glucose during this period.

There is one physiologic secret of exercise fueling that needs to be underscored and practiced by every youth or adult engaged in exercise, whether recreational or professional. It is:

Glucokinase must be unlocked from the liver cell and available to allow for glucose uptake by the liver during exercise. Exercise inhibits glucokinase release, but fructose will release this enzyme. Fueling during exercise with fructose and glucose in a balanced ratio facilitates glucose uptake into the liver and promotes glycogen formation. The result is improved power output, improved mental acuity, improved psychology and improved recovery. And with improved recovery comes the added bonus of improved overall health.

By now, you will have discovered just what fuel accomplishes that. Honey is that ideal fuel. Sports drinks without a balance of glucose and fructose will hydrate you, but they cannot release glucokinase and facilitate liver glycogen formation as honey does.

Refueling in the post-exercise period has two main considerations: to replenish depleted fuel stores and to ready the body for recovery. Replenishment of muscle glycogen is easily achieved with carbohydrate drinks or food, such as whole grain breads, pasta, rice and potatoes – these foods are glucose based and the metabolic environment at this period is optimal for muscle replenishment. In the immediate post-exercise period, usually lasting about 2 hours, uptake of protein is optimized. It makes good sense to take advantage of this by consuming lean meat, chicken or fish. The replenishment of muscle glycogen is improved when carbohydrates are ingested during this period along with protein.

The post-exercise refueling period must also give attention to replenishing the liver glycogen stores. This will occur if you include some fructose-containing foods, such as fruits and vegetables or *honey*, which ensure that the liver takes in and stores glucose. However, any liver glycogen formed will be quickly released from the liver during this period to provide glucose for depleted muscle tissue.

Refueling for recovery is most critical during the period just before bedtime, when recovery physiology is the key metabolic consideration. The most critical consideration during this time is the liver glycogen status. If you assume that the post-exercise refueling from foods, beverages and/or supplements is adequate to replenish muscle glycogen storage, and you have included protein and fats to provide the building materials necessary for repair and reconstruction of tissues, then the last and vital consideration is that of selective replenishment of the liver glycogen store. An adequate liver glycogen store is foundational to provide the optimal metabolic environment for recovery physiology during sleep.

Don't Be Confused About Energy

There are many "energy drinks" and "energy boosters" on the market these days, and most of them promise to "release energy." Remember, there is a difference between *releasing* energy and *providing* energy. Many substances will release energy into the blood stream; caffeine is the best example of this. Caffeine is a thermogenic (literally heat-producing) drug. It increases the metabolic rate and prompts the release of fatty acids into the blood stream. Unfortunately, most of these fatty acids return to the fat stores after exercise and contribute little toward energy requirements.

The primary energy source used by the body for exercise is glucose. As the intensity of exercise increases, the higher the ratio of glucose-to-fat is burned. The best possible energy-providing food is honey. Not only does honey provide the correct balance of fructose to glucose, but it will also optimally and selectively refuel the liver without a significant digestive burden during the post-exercise recovery. This is an important consideration, as digestion is a metabolically expensive and energy-demanding series of physiologic processes. The amount of honey necessary after exercise and before rest periods will vary according to body size and the status of liver glycogen stores. Typically, 1 or 2 tablespoons will provide optimum fuel to ensure adequate liver glycogen during recovery times. And when adequate liver glycogen stores are available during rest, fat burning will be optimized.

Honey is the highest-octane natural fuel available to humans for exercise and recovery!

Ten Basic Facts for Exercise Fueling
1. The primary fuel for exercise in humans is glucose, a simple carbohydrate.
2. The greater the intensity of exercise, the higher the percentage of glucose burned relative to fat.

3. The most significant energy storehouse for exercise and recovery is the liver glycogen store.

4. Fueling for muscles and liver should be undertaken before, during, and after exercise, and with respect to the liver glycogen reserve, prior to recovery sleep.

5. Fructose is the sugar specifically selected by the liver to facilitate and regulate glucose uptake.

6. A fructose-based fuel (like fruit, fruit juice or *honey*) during exercise will increase oxidation and therefore increase power output.

7. Optimal fueling of both the muscles and the liver will reduce production of adrenal stress hormones and protect muscle proteins from degradation.

8. Optimal fueling is as important during training as it is for competition. In one sense it is more important, because it is the daily metabolic toll during training that will impact the athlete's health over his/her competitive life, both in the short and long term.

9. Fats are never a limiting factor during exercise; they are abundantly available. Any attempt to release extra fats during exercise will be counterproductive and promote long-term negative consequences.

10. Proteins may be a significant fuel used during exercise, but good fueling protocols must take the liver into account. The liver glycogen storehouse is critical.

Honey for Alcohol Detoxification and Liver Health

Repeatedly throughout this book we have focused on the role of honey as an ideal source of liver glycogen, which is available to fuel the brain during times when the brain is at greatest risk from low fuel reserves such as during exercise and sleep. Another time when the brain is at risk is during and immediately following the consumption of alcohol.

Alcohol is a powerful oxidant. It is detoxified primarily in the liver. When consumed, it forces the liver into immediate action to combat potential damage from free radical accumulation. In addition, alcohol has a hypoglycemic effect on the system, driving down blood glucose levels. When drinking excessively, brain metabolism slows, cognitive function declines, speech becomes slurred and incoherent, and the resultant extreme metabolic stress of continued alcohol intake may lead to coma, especially in young people.

One of the best-kept secrets about honey is its ability to facilitate the detoxification of alcohol and protect the liver from toxic damage associated with alcohol consumption. While we are not in any way attempting to justify or excuse excess alcohol consumption, it is advised to consider the facts presented in this section the next time you have a few drinks.

The enzyme responsible for detoxifying alcohol in the liver is known as alcohol dehydrogenase. It is the action of this enzyme that converts alcohol to acetaldehyde and then to acetic acid. These reactions quickly use up available supplies of the enzyme nicotinomide adenine dinucleotide (NAD), which is reduced to NADH in the process. The amount of NAD available is the rate-limiting factor in the pathway of alcohol detoxification.

When honey is consumed, fructose comes to the rescue of a stressed liver and rapidly recycles the reduced enzyme NADH back to NAD, restarting the cycle and allowing for more alcohol to be detoxified.[180] In addition, honey is packed with a wonderful array of antioxidants, which will provide protection against the free radical attack on liver and other cells in the body.

Several papers published by Dr. Noori Al-Waili have demonstrated the benefits of honey consumption on the liver, both protecting and preserving liver function.[181, 182] The author concluded that "exclusive honey feeding (using only 50% concentration of honey) significantly modifies and ameliorates biochemical and hematological changes . . ." within the body. The next time you are thinking about potentially harming your liver with alcohol consumption, be wise and take a tablespoon of honey before and after you drink. You will do your liver and yourself a favor.

Honey and Infants

Many honey packers place a warning on honey containers that reads: "Honey is not recommended for use in infants less than one year of age." The reason for this warning is supposedly linked to the risk of botulism from eating raw honey. This is partially correct. While there is a remote possibility that botulism spores from the bacterium *Clostridium botulinum* may exist in honey,[183] the likelihood that an infant will contract botulism from breast-feeding is greater than the risk from getting botulism from consuming honey.[184] Botulism spores are everywhere. Since 1970, more than 1000 cases of infant botulism in this country have been reported to the Centers for Disease Control and Prevention (CDC). Some studies have confirmed that the ingestion of honey was indeed responsible, but in the majority of cases, honey consumption was proven not to be the cause.

Honey is a natural or raw food and may contain botulism spores. Though botulism spores produce harmful toxins only when they grow, they cannot grow in honey. Neither can the bacteria itself grow in honey. Nevertheless, honey, like any raw or unprocessed food, may contain spores and the presence of these spores is potentially dangerous to infants whose immune systems are not mature.

The issue, therefore, is at what age is an infant's immune system mature enough to deal with many kinds of antigens and other potentially harmful proteins. The answer is generally about 12 months of age. Raw foods of any kind, including honey, are not recommended for infants with immature immune systems. Some infants' immune systems will mature earlier, some later. Older children with fully developed immune systems are able to neutralize this bacterium and its potentially harmful spores. Therefore, the wise course of action is not to feed raw foods, including honey, to an infant whose immune system has not reached maturity.

Honey and Aging

Some would argue that the afflictions of aging cannot be prevented, or that it is too late for prevention; treatment is the only option. The increasing number of prescriptive medicines taken every day by the elderly only serves to illustrate and confirm this belief.

The unfortunate fact is that it may be too late for preventive strategies for some. Lifelong habits of dietary abuses and lifestyle choices have reaped certain rewards.

However, for many, perhaps the great majority, the following suggestions (or "directives") can be put in place today that will produce months and years of healthy life. They carry no risk, produce no side effects, are drug free, and cost but pennies a day. And while they may not cure all of one's diseases, their implementation will bring about positive changes in one's health in a matter of days or weeks, regardless of age.

Directives for Better Health

1. **Don't go to bed hungry**! Avoidance of food in the hours before bedtime ensures certain metabolic disaster during the nocturnal fast.
2. **Give your liver a chance to make and store glycogen not only before bedtime but also throughout the day.** (Adequate liver glycogen formation will not come from continuing to consume excessive amounts of sugar and high-fructose corn syrup.) Avoid liver glycogen depletion!
3. **Eliminate excess sucrose and HFCS from your diet.** These foods (and processed foods that contain them) only raise blood sugar levels and result in excessive insulin secretion (hyperinsulinemia). Excess glucose and fructose get stored as fat.
4. **Keep your brain content by providing it with fuel first.** When the brain is content, the whole body is content! Remember that the brain depends primarily on liver glycogen for fuel, and a well-fueled brain prevents metabolic stress.
5. **Adopt a simple strategy of consuming honey every day**: a tablespoon or more

at bedtime, a tablespoon in the morning with breakfast, and one or two during the day before and after periods of exercise.

These simple suggestions will result in one or more of the following benefits:

1. You will sleep better and longer, as the insomnia caused by metabolic stress will be eliminated. Restorative sleep will be enhanced and recovery physiology will occur without interruption throughout the night.
2. Your sleep patterns will include more frequent periods of REM sleep. Your dreams will be more vivid and your dream recall remarkable.
3. Your mental acuity and memory recall will improve.
4. Your blood sugar levels will stabilize (the highs and lows will be eliminated), and your food cravings will gradually go away. (If you are diabetic, your HbA_{1c} levels will decrease.)
5. You will awaken in the morning feeling more rested and without feelings of intense hunger, shakiness, nausea, or weakness.
6. Your total cholesterol and triglyceride levels will come down, and your HDL (high-density lipoproteins, or "good") cholesterol level will increase gradually.
7. You may lose a little weight, but perhaps more importantly, you will burn more body fat during the night to fuel the

normal recovery and restoration of body tissues that occur during rest.

8. The inflammatory processes that accompany aging will become less intense and symptomatic.

9. Risk factors for all of the diseases of aging that are associated with chronic inflammation will gradually be reduced.

Honey: the All-star Super Food

"You've changed my life!" exclaimed a friend from our church choir one Sunday morning. (She had received a copy of *The Honey Revolution* as a gift.) What she had experienced was a dramatic improvement in quality and duration of sleep over the past few weeks simply by ingesting a tablespoon of honey before bedtime. The fact that honey improves sleep is truly an astounding and revolutionary benefit. A full store of liver glycogen at bedtime insures adequate fuel for the brain during the night fast and avoids the onset of metabolic (adrenal-driven) stress during the early morning hours. This simple intervention has produced amazing results for many.

The anecdotal reports of vivid dreams and increased dream recall from many are evidence of an increase in REM sleep by taking a bit of honey before bedtime. REM sleep frequency and duration decreases with aging, but honey consumption at bedtime appears to reverse this trend, thus affecting not only sleep patterns, but also a host of other conditions associated with poor quality sleep.

Not everyone who consumes honey at bedtime will lose weight, but many do. Some report that the simple addition of a tablespoon of honey taken at bedtime is the only thing to which they can attribute the loss of several pounds over a few months. One couple reported a combined 85-pound weight loss over a period of 6 months. These stories are also consistent with animal studies that show weight loss as a common result of being fed a diet based on honey rather than sucrose or HFCS.

The reductions in blood sugar, cholesterol and triglycerides, and the reduced risks of the associated conditions of diabetes, cardiovascular disease, Alzheimer's disease, and other conditions included in the metabolic syndrome potentially impacted by the simple strategy of consuming honey add to the list of seemingly miraculous interventions brought about by this strategy.

What does this all mean in real cost savings? Is it possible to estimate what a simple dietary change can do? What if only a small fraction of the population adopted this strategy? Is it possible to know what the potential outcomes might be?

Calculations of cost effectiveness and/or cost benefit analysis for any intervention strategy in healthcare is challenging, given the number of variables, individual differences, overlapping diagnoses, and multiple outcomes which must be factored in to arrive at credible numbers. Just for the sake of discussion, take a look at the real costs of several of the diseases for which honey may provide a therapeutic benefit.

Annual Direct and Projected Costs of Several Diseases in United States

Disease or Condition	Direct Costs	Year
Obesity	$190.2 billion	2010
Childhood Obesity	$14 billion	2010
Diabetes	$245 billion	2012
Hyperlipidemia	$38.5 billion	2010
Heart Disease	$108.9 billion	2011
Cardiovascular disease	$312.6 billion	2011
Cancer	$124.6 billion	2010
Alzheimer's disease	$203 billion	2013

The total direct costs for the diseases and conditions shown in the table above are staggering, totaling over $1 trillion per year. Yet what is even more staggering is the projected rise in these costs over the next few decades. For example, by 2050, the direct cost of Alzheimer's disease alone is projected to be $1.2 trillion.

Public health initiatives involving education and/ or some treatment intervention typically target a reduction in cost or reduction in disease incidence or prevalence. As an example, what if it were suggested that adopting a strategy of consuming honey, both at bedtime and during the day, would reduce the incidence of the diseases listed in the table by only 1% across the entire population of the United States. That would represent a potential savings of over $10 billion per year in direct costs. Now, what if only 10% of the population adopted this strategy. The resultant savings would still be over $1 billion per year. Not a bad return for a simple strategy that has no risks, produces no side effects or negative health consequences, and costs less than $20 per month per person.

No doubt, the beekeepers and honey producers have already done the math. If 10% of the population of the United States were to consume an average of 4 tablespoons of honey per day, it would take more than 6 times the amount of honey produced each year *in the entire world*, just to meet the demand.

How Much Honey Is Enough?

The optimum recommended daily consumption of honey is 3 to 5 tablespoons taken in divided doses. This equates to approximately 54 to 90 grams per day, providing about 200 to 360 calories. For best results, 1 to 2 tablespoons of honey should be consumed just before bedtime. The amount may depend on what was eaten and the time between supper and bedtime. In other words, did the evening meal consist of foods that contributed to the liver glycogen store? Another tablespoon should be consumed with breakfast, along with some protein, fruit, and juice. This is the best way to refill the empty liver glycogen tank, following 8 hours of sleep.

During the day, honey consumption depends on activity level and timing of meals. If you exercise during the day, a tablespoon of honey before and after a workout is a good way to prevent the onset of metabolic stress. These and many more suggestions of how to eat in order to fuel the brain are given in *Feed Your Brain First*, along with recipes and menu plans that will ensure that the brain does not go without fuel throughout the day and night.

Remember to buy and consume raw, unfiltered honey, preferably from beekeepers or honey producers that you know.[185] What do you have to lose, except a few pounds? What do you have to gain, except significant reduction in risks for many diseases? Join *The Honey Revolution*. You and your family will share the benefits of honey experienced by thousands of others.

Glenn's Story – A Happy Ending

(Adapted from *Feed Your Brain First, The Honey Revolution – Part 3*)

G lenn was just a few days past his 77th birthday when he handed me an envelope. Inside were three pages of lab results from his recent physical exam and four pages from his physical exam exactly one year ago. His smile gave indication that something good was about to be revealed.

Several months before, I had shared with Glenn and his wife Sandy, the principles of brain fueling – eat foods that have a balance of fructose and glucose in order to produce more liver glycogen; don't go to bed hungry; limit the consumption of starchy, glucose-rich foods; and consume more honey, especially at bedtime and in the morning.

Glenn had reason to be concerned. He was a pilot and though his flying was now limited to occasional trips in his twin engine Cessna, he subjected himself to the mandatory annual flight physicals required of someone his age. A year ago, his lab work revealed an elevated cholesterol level (237 mg/dL – normal being below 199 mg/dL) with the LDL-cholesterol fraction markedly elevated (162 mg/dL – normal being below 99 mg/dL). His triglycerides were normal but at the upper limit of the normal range. His doctor recommended lipid-lowering drugs, which Glenn had taken for a while, but later abandoned due to the unpleasant side effects.

A few weeks before his scheduled flight physical, Glenn asked if I thought honey would help with his cholesterol lab values. My answer was an unqualified "Yes."

A few days before his appointment, Glenn checked with me again, this time to ask how honey might affect his fasting blood sugar. My response was that fasting blood sugar readings are typically elevated due to what is known as the "dawn phenomenon." The brain, sensing that its fuel supply is low or depleted after several hours of fasting (such as overnight), initiates adrenal-driven stress resulting in new glucose being formed from amino acids. Thus the blood sugar reading after an overnight fast is always going to be artificially elevated.

My suggestion to Glenn was to have his tablespoon of honey at bedtime and again in the morning an hour or so before his blood samples were to be drawn. Though this advice might seem counter-intuitive to some, and was contrary to his doctor's instructions regarding fasting, Glenn did as I suggested.

The results were in. The envelope opened. Now it was my turn to smile. Glenn's total cholesterol was 175 mg/dL, down from 237 mg/dL, a drop of 62 mg/dL. His LDL-cholesterol was down from 162 mg/dL to 113 mg/dL, and though still slightly elevated, not something that warranted intervention. In addition, Glenn's VLDL (Very Low Density Lipoprotein) was down from 26 mg/dL to 14 mg/dL. Though neither value was elevated, the drop was significant.

Even more remarkable was his triglyceride level. A year ago, Glenn's triglyceride level was 131 mg/dL. This year it was 69 mg/dL, a drop of 62 mg/dL.

While both readings were within the "normal range," this dramatic reduction was further indication of the therapeutic effects of adding regular "doses" of honey to one's diet.

An understanding of the metabolism of honey as detailed throughout this book would indicate that Glenn's dramatic results should not be viewed with surprise. Yet, Glenn's physician remained unconvinced. The same can be said for a majority of physicians today who practice by the numbers, and "treat the numbers" with a host of costly prescription drugs that, while they may bring the numbers down, do nothing for the underlying cause of the condition.

Is Glenn's metabolic response to consuming honey typical? Is this something that can be expected by everyone? Although the research confirmation so far comes from limited animal and human studies, much anecdotal evidence is being accumulated that would answer these questions affirmatively. Dozens of folks have written to me and shared similar results.

The good news is that one does not need to wait to join *The Honey Revolution*. There are no risks, side effects or negative health consequences from starting today. You may not have the dramatic results that Glenn did in such a short time, but it is quite likely that you will experience better health and reduced risks of suffering the consequences of all the metabolic conditions discussed in this book.

UPDATE: A year had elapsed since I last heard from Glenn concerning his lab results. Again, he provided me with lab results from this year's annual exam. Admittedly, he had not been as faithful with regular doses of honey at bedtime. His total cholesterol was up a bit, as were his triglycerides, yet still within the normal range. His HDL cholesterol (good cholesterol) had inched up from 48 to 51 and his coronary risk ratio (total cholesterol divided by the HDL cholesterol) had gone from 3.65 to 4.29, still well within the "negative risk factor" range.

If any conclusion can be reached from Glenn's experience, it is this: Honey consumption is not something to start a few days or weeks before one's annual physical exam. Honey consumption needs to be a lifetime habit for best results.

FINAL GOOD WORD

In the Old Testament book of Deuteronomy, Moses includes an expansive song citing God's abundant nutritional provisions for the children of Israel.

> *"He made then ride over the highlands; he let them feast on the crops of the fields. He nourished them with* **honey** *from the cliffs, with olive oil from the hard rock."* (Deuteronomy 32:13, New Living Translation)

May you also experience these abundant blessings and enjoy years of good health.

FREQUENTLY ASKED QUESTIONS

(Adapted from *The Honey Revolution – Abridged*)

The section presents information in a simple question-and-answer format edited to be simple and concise. References and citations for the facts contained herein may be found in any of *The Honey Revolution* book series.

Q: *What is honey?*

A: Honey is a natural, sweet substance, made from the nectar of flowering plants and trees by honeybees, to which nothing has been added and nothing taken away. It is composed of nearly equal proportions of the simple sugars fructose and glucose, plus small amounts of other sugars, and is about 18% water. Over 180 different substances have been identified in honey, including 5 enzymes, 6 vitamins, 8 lipids, trace amounts of 12 minerals and 17 elements, 18 different acids, 18 amino acids (proteins), 18 bioflavonoids, and 26 aroma compounds. Currently, there are more than 300 varietals of honey produced in the United States.

Q: *How many calories are there in a tablespoon of honey?*

A: One tablespoon (21 grams) of honey provides 64 calories, primarily from carbohydrates or sugars.

Q: *If half of the sugar found in honey is fructose, isn't that a lot? Isn't fructose supposed to be bad for you?*

A: Fructose, also known as "fruit sugar," is not harmful to your health if consumed in the small amounts typically found in fruits, some vegetables, and honey. Each tablespoon of honey contains an average of 8 grams of fructose on average, the same amount found in one small apple. Fructose is essential for the liver to create and store glucose as glycogen.

Q: *So, what's the problem with fructose that I keep hearing about?*

A: The major problem with fructose is the amount that is consumed each day. The average American, consumes more than a third of a pound of sucrose and HFCS, each day. Sucrose is half fructose and HFCS is typically 55% fructose. That much fructose simply overwhelms the liver, which is the main place in the body where fructose can be metabolized. Some fructose gets converted to glucose in the liver and stored as glycogen. When confronted with more fructose than it can handle, the liver stops everything else that it is doing to break down the fructose, which is converted into fatty acids and released into the circulation to be carried to fat tissue throughout the body and stored as fat. This amount of fructose consumption is the main reason we have an epidemic of obesity in the United States.

Q: *How does the fructose in honey help the liver store glucose?*

A: Fructose unlocks the enzyme hidden in the liver cell nuclei that is necessary to convert glucose to glycogen. (This enzyme is called glucokinase.) When fructose and glucose are present together, fructose assists the liver in taking glucose out of the circulation. This effectively lowers blood sugar by removing glucose from the blood stream and bringing it into the liver, where it is converted to glycogen and stored. Without fructose, glucose passes through the liver and into the blood, triggering the release of insulin. Insulin drives glucose into the cells where it is used as energy or stored as fat.

Q: *Is there a difference between glucose stored in the muscle cells as glycogen and the glycogen stored in the liver?*

A: Both muscle glycogen and liver glycogen are made up of multiple glucose molecules joined together into chains. Though they are the same in substance, there is a big difference between the two in how they get used in the body. Once glucose enters the muscle cells and is formed into glycogen, it does not come out. Muscle cells trap it there for later use or convert it to fat. Liver glycogen, on the other hand, can be easily converted back to glucose and shared with other cells and organs of the body when needed for energy, especially the red blood cells, the kidneys, and the brain.

Q: *Why is it important to maintain a reserve of glycogen in the liver?*

A: Liver glycogen is the primary source of fuel reserve for the brain. During sleep and during exercise, the brain is at risk of running out of fuel. During both of those times, the liver glycogen store provides fuel for the brain's energy needs. Without adequate liver glycogen, the brain initiates a form of metabolic stress to provide fuel for itself.

Q: *How much glycogen can the liver store?*
A: The liver can only store about 75 grams of glycogen at any one time. In some individuals, the liver capacity for glycogen may be as low as 50 grams or as high as 120 grams. The exact capacity of the liver glycogen store is difficult to measure directly but may be estimated by other indicators.

Q: *How much glycogen does the liver release as glucose for the body during rest?*
A: At rest, the liver releases 10 grams of glucose per hour: 6.5 grams for the brain, and 3.5 grams for the kidneys and red blood cells. That means that the brain only has enough glucose from the liver for 7 to 8 hours.

Q: *How much glycogen is released from the liver during exercise?*
A: During exercise, the liver may release glucose at a rate of up to 100 grams per hour, depending on the intensity of the exercise. That means that the brain can survive for about 45 minutes until it needs to refuel.

Q: *Does the brain have any other source of fuel?*
A: Yes. The brain will burn some amino acids from proteins. After several days of starvation, the brain will also begin to burn ketones (organic compounds) derived from fats. However, the primary source of fuel for the brain is glucose from the blood and from the liver. The brain cells contain only enough fuel to survive about 30 seconds, and there is enough glucose in the blood (blood sugar) at any one time for the brain to survive about 30 minutes.

Q: *What happens when the brain runs out of fuel?*

A: If that were to happen, one would lapse into a coma and eventually die. But the brain protects itself so that it will not run out of fuel. It does this by initiating metabolic stress.

Q: *What is metabolic stress?*

A: Metabolic stress is a protective mechanism initiated by the brain when it senses its fuel reserve in the liver is running low — sort of like the "low fuel" light coming on in your car when the gas tank is near empty. When this happens, the brain triggers the adrenal glands to release adrenalin and cortisol. These hormones then mobilize alternative fuel stores, such as fatty acids and protein from muscle tissue. The protein from muscle tissue gets broken down into amino acids that are carried back to the liver, where they are converted to new glucose for the brain. Metabolic stress is sometimes referred to as the "fight or flight" reaction. The intent is to protect the fuel supply for the brain.

Q: *Does metabolic stress ever occur at night as we sleep?*

A: Absolutely and frequently for many of us. When we go to bed without replenishing our liver glycogen store, there may only be enough glycogen supply in the liver to fuel the brain for four to five hours.

Q: *What does metabolic stress do if it happens during sleep?*

A: It does the same thing as when it happens during waking hours; adrenalin and cortisol are released. Adrenalin raises our heart rate and blood pressure and wakes us up; cortisol triggers a host of other changes in our resting physiology that preserve and create an adequate glucose supply for the brain. The end result is that our sleep is interrupted until the brain is assured of having a sufficient fuel supply to allow sleep to continue.

Q: *Does consuming honey before bedtime prevent metabolic stress from happening?*

A: Yes, indeed! Honey, with its ideal ratio of fructose to glucose, allows for immediate glycogen formation in the liver ("tops off the tank"). When the liver glycogen store is full, the brain has enough fuel to get through the night without interruption. Honey "energizes" the brain for rest.

Q: *Will eating other foods prevent metabolic stress?*

A: Yes, but with consequences. A small portion of fruit (about one cup) contains about the same amount of fructose and glucose as 1 tablespoon of honey. A small serving of some vegetables also contains similar amounts of glucose and fructose. However, eating fruits and vegetables before bedtime adds to the work of the digestive tract at a time when it is being "powered down" in preparation for rest.

Some vegetables also contain a large amount of starch, another carbohydrate, which is immediately converted to glucose in our stomach and small intestine. As it enters the blood stream, this glucose causes a big release of insulin, which drives glucose into the muscle cells and removes it from circulation, keeping it from the brain. Within a couple of hours, our blood sugar level falls and causes metabolic stress. A small amount of honey (1 to 2 tablespoons) is the best food with which to restock the liver glycogen store before bed.

Q: *Won't honey raise my blood sugar also?*

A: A small dose of honey does not raise blood sugar as much as an equivalent dose of glucose or sugar (sucrose); it does not trigger a large insulin spike. Honey controls or regulates blood sugar and helps to stabilize it within a normal range.

Q: *Does honey do anything else to help me sleep?*
A: Yes. The glucose portion of honey does trigger a small insulin release. Insulin in the blood causes a substance called tryptophan to be driven into the brain, where it is converted to serotonin. Serotonin promotes relaxation. In total darkness, serotonin is converted to melatonin, which then activates sleep. This is what we call the HoneY-MelatoniN (HYMN) Cycle.

Q: *You said earlier that honey "energizes" my brain for rest. I thought my brain needed to sleep, not be energized during rest. What about that?*
A: Sleep is actually a high-energy state for the brain. During sleep, the brain requires as much fuel as when it is awake (some researchers say it needs even more). When you go to sleep, your brain goes to work. Providing energy for the brain during rest allows it to accomplish or control the normal functions of recovery, memory consolidation and learning, immune system improvements, and other benefits of restorative sleep. Without sufficient fuel reserves for the brain during eight hours of rest, sleep will be interrupted, and metabolic stress will be initiated by the brain to ensure adequate fuel for itself.

Q: *Can you describe two significant things that regular honey consumption will do?*
A: Certainly! First, eating honey on a regular basis (3 to 5 tablespoons a day) helps to regulate blood sugar

within a normal range and produce and store the liver glycogen needed to fuel the brain. Second, eating 1 to 2 tablespoons of honey before bedtime will result in quality sleep that promotes the occurrence of recovery physiology during the nighttime and eliminates the need for the brain to activate metabolic stress.

Q: *What will eating honey do for all the conditions and diseases related to metabolic stress?*

A: The fact that honey helps to prevent metabolic stress by providing fuel for the brain means that it will also reduce the risks for the conditions and diseases associated with the metabolic syndrome, including obesity, diabetes, hypertension, thyroid conditions, and others described in this book.

Q: *Does honey prevent metabolic stress for everyone?*

A: The principles of how honey is metabolized (forms liver glycogen directly, fuels the brain, and reduces metabolic stress) are the same for everyone. However, each person's metabolism is a bit different and is subject to individual, environmental, and genetic factors that may modify or limit the effects of honey consumption. The good news is that the consumption of honey daily in small amounts daily has no side affects, comes with no risks, and may be safely tried by anyone including infants over 12 months of age.

Q: *How long will it take for me to experience the effects of honey?*

A: Within a few days, sleep patterns will change and dreams will be more vivid, indicating more restful sleep. And within 2 to 3 weeks, blood sugar levels will be more regulated, which will be more obvious to some who are used to experiencing extreme highs and lows. Other changes, such as reductions in the levels of cholesterol and triglycerides may take several weeks. Lowered risks for many of the conditions and diseases mentioned in this book will be evident over a lifetime. It's not too late to get started.

ENDNOTES

Foreword

[1] During the century from 1911 through 2010, the number of research studies involving honey has grown from less than five per year to well over 700 per year according to PubMed.gov, a service of the U.S. National Library of Medicine, National Institutes of Health.

[2] *The Honey Revolution* series includes: *The Honey Revolution – Restoring the Health of Future Generations*, Ron Fessenden, MD, MPH and Mike McInnes, MRPS, WorldClassEmprise, LLC (2008); *The Honey Revolution – Abridged*, Ron Fessenden, MD, MPH and Mike McInnes, MRPS, WorldClassEmprise, LLC (2010); *Feed Your Brain First*, Ron Fessenden, MD, MPH, TGBTG-Books, LLC (2013).

The Honey Revolution: Changing the Way We Think About Honey

[3] These sugars are called oligosaccharides, such as fructooligosaccharide, a compound sugar made up of several molecules of fructose joined together.

[4] Health benefit information from research studies cited throughout this book applies to natural unfiltered honey

or specific honey varietals. Processed and blended honey may or may not provide similar benefits. Further study is needed to determine if health benefits are applicable to processed honey.

[5] IM Paul, MD, *et al*, "Effect of Honey, Dextromethorphan, and No Treatment on Nocturnal Cough and Sleep Quality for Coughing Children and Their Parents." *Arch Pediatr Adolesc Med* 2007; 161(12): 1140-1146.

[6] *Helicobactor pylori* (or *H. pylori*) is the specific bacteria that causes gastric ulcers.

[7] Tupelo honey, produced in several Southern states, is one specific honey varietal that does not crystallize, probably because of its higher fructose content.

[8] One particular varietal of honey produced in Hawaii from the blossoms of the Kiawe Tree found on Maui and in the Puako region of the Big Island crystallizes rapidly, on its own without any artificial processing, into a creamy white honey.

The Case for a Honey Standard

[9] Eva Crane, PhD, *Honey A Comprehensive Survey*. Crane, Russak & Company, Inc. New York (1975).

[10] L Birkman, *et al*, "Clarifying the Status of Pollen in Honey." Document created by request of the European Parliament's Committee on the Environment, Public Health and Food Safety, September 2013.

[11] The actual wording of a portion of the adopted recommendations is as follows: In section 3.1 titled "Essential Composition and Quality Factors," the recommendation was to "*remove the wording* 'nor shall any other additions be made other than honey' and 'no constituent particular to honey may be removed or changed'" *(emphasis added)*. In section 6 titled "Labeling," the recommendation was to *remove the "entire section" (emphasis added)*.

Health Benefits or Health Claims – Is There a Difference

[12] The bee products industry in the United States has witnessed such penalties being enforced by the FDA regarding claims made about the use of bee pollen.

[13] R Dhingra, MD, *et al*, "Soft Drink Consumption and Risk of Developing Cardiometabolic Risk Factors and the Metabolic Syndrome in Middle-aged Adults in the Community." *Circulation: Journal of the American Heart Association* July 31, 2007.

[14] *New Scientist* magazine, Issue 2619, September 4, 2007, page 7.

[15] T Waldron, "Sugary Sodas High in Diabetes-linked Compound." www.healthfinder.gov, a service of the US Department of Health and Human Services.

[16] ME Bocarsly, "High-fructose Corn Syrup Causes Characteristics of Obesity in Rats: Increased Body Weight, Body Fat and Triglyceride Levels." www.NIH.gov. National Institutes of Health, Nov 2010.

[17] The reasons for this are clear when considering what Joe Traynor said in *Honey, the Gourmet Medicine* (Kovak Books, 2002), "Honey is a medicine without profit." Furthermore, there are over 300 varietals of honey available in the U.S., making generalized statements about the health benefits of honey difficult, if not impossible, given the specific constraints of research protocols.

[18] The metabolic syndrome in some expanded definitions includes the following diseases and conditions: adult and childhood obesity, type 2 diabetes, cardiovascular disease, arrhythmia, hypertension, stroke, osteoporosis, hypothyroidism, depression, Alzheimer's disease, dementia, and sleep disorders.

[19] A Samanta, AC Burden, GR Jones, "Plasma glucose responses to glucose, sucrose, and honey in patients with

diabetes mellitus: an analysis of glycaemic and peak incremental indices," *Diabet Med,* 1985 Sep; 2(5): 371-3.

[20] Phil Shambaugh, Virginia Worthington and John H. Herbert, "Differential Effects of Honey, Sucrose, and Fructose on Blood Sugar Levels," *J Manip Physiol Thera* (1990) 13: 322.

[21] Noori S. Al-Waili, "Natural Honey Lowers Plasma Glucose, C-Reactive Protein, Homocysteine, and Blood Lipids in Healthy, Diabetic, and Hyperlipidemic Subjects: Comparison with Dextrose and Sucrose," *J Med Food* (2004) 7: 100.

[22] Omotayo Erejuwa, Siti Sulaiman, and Mohd Wahab, "Oligosaccharides Might Contribute to the Antidiabetic Effect of Honey: A Review of Literature," *Molecules 2012,* 17: 248-266.

Honey: More Than Just a Sweetener

[23] The most logical explanation for this observed phenomenon seems to be that honey consumption works independently of insulin in reducing blood sugar. Honey is rapidly absorbed into the blood and from there quickly transported into the liver cells where is it stored as glycogen, thus removing it from the blood, thereby triggering a lesser insulin response and a lesser dependence on insulin production from the pancreas.

Tom's Story

[24] It is well documented in scientific literature that excessive consumption of HFCS contributes to the production of triglycerides, which are then stored in the liver resulting a condition that pathologists call a "fatty liver."
[25] Liver glycogen is the one critical reserve fuel for the brain, red blood cells and the kidneys. Liver glycogen

also serves as a reserve fuel for every other cell in the body when blood sugar is low. At rest, a normal liver can release up to ten grams of glucose per hour for the rest of the body to help meet its metabolic needs.

[26] *Chronic brain starvation* is repeated brain starvation that occurs nightly when the liver glycogen reserve becomes depleted during sleep. *Chronic sleep loss* occurs as a result of brain starvation that triggers the release of adrenalin and cortisol resulting in interrupted and short sleep. *Chronic metabolic stress* is associated with repeated and excessive adrenalin and cortisol release. It is a protective mechanism initiated by the brain to provide fuel for itself when liver glycogen reserves are depleted.

Is Your Dietary Shift Showing?

[27] Cited from the American Diabetes Association research for the year 2012 released on March 6, 2013. This figure represents a 41% increase over a five-year period.

[28] Refined sugar from beet and cane is sucrose, made up of equal portions of glucose and fructose. HFCS is nearly equal portions of glucose and fructose, depending on the specific ratio used by food processors (either 48:52 or 45:55).

[29] *Arch Inter Med* 1992; 152: 1371-1372.

[30] GD Lawrence, "Dietary fats and health: dietary recommendations in the context of scientific evidence." *Adv Nutr* (2013) 4: 294-302.

[31] Simple sugars (monosaccharides) found in natural foods are typically found in pairs, such as glucose and fructose, or lactose (a disaccharide in milk products), which is actually two simple sugars, glucose and galactose joined together in a single molecule. The near 1:1 ratio of these sugar pairs makes a big difference in how they are metabolized in the body.

[32] Last updated by the USDA, May 2013.

[33] GA Bray, *et al*, "Consumption of High-fructose Corn Syrup in Beverages May Play a Role in the Epidemic of Obesity," *American Journal of Clinical Nutrition*, Vol. 79, No. 4, 537-543, April 2004.

[34] Finally, after nearly forty years of silence!

[35] HbA1c (hemoglobin A1c) or glycated hemoglobin is a form of hemoglobin to which glucose molecules become attached. HbA1c is used to identify the average blood glucose concentration over a period of weeks prior to the time the lab test is taken. A normal HbA1c measurement is considered to be $\leq 6.5\%$.

[36] The normal range for blood glucose (blood sugar) in the human is considered to be between 70 and 110 mg/dL or approximately 4–6 mmol/L.

[37] Starch is a polysaccharide made up of many molecules of glucose. Plants make starch as a way of storing sugar for energy for growth and reproduction.

Differentiating Honey from Other Sweeteners

[38] Q Yang, PhD, *et al*, "Added Sugar Intake and Cardio-vascular Diseases Mortality Among US Adults." *JAMA Intern Med*. Published online February 03, 2014.

[39] Townsend Letter for Doctors, March 1993

[40] JD McPherson, *et al*, "Role of Fructose in Glycation ...," *Biochemistry* 27 (5): 1901-7, November 1988.

[41] B Levi and MJ Werman, "Long-term Fructose Consumption Accelerates Glycation ... " *Journal of Nutrition* 128: 1442-9 (1998).

[42] H Jurgens, *et al*, "Consuming Fructose-sweetened Beverages Increases Body Adiposity ... " *Obesity Research* 13 (7): 1146-1156 (2005).

[43] JP Bantle, *et al*, "Effects of Dietary Fructose on Plasma Lipids . . . " *American Journal of Clinical Nutrition* 72 (5): 1128 -1134 (November 2000).

[44] X Ouyang, MD, *et al*, "Fructose Consumption as a Risk Factor for Non-alcoholic Fatty Liver Disease." *J Hetatol* 48 (6): 993-999, June 2008.

[45] K Melanson, *et al*, "Eating Rate and Satiation." Obesity Society (NAASO) 2006 Annual Meeting, October 20-24, 2006, Boston, Massachusetts.

[46] This is known as the *"fructose paradox"* described in *The Honey Revolution* (2008).

[47] It is estimated that the daily consumption of glucose is five times that of fructose.

[48] As an example, a 32-ounce soft drink beverage contains over 75 grams of fructose alone.

[49] A Samanta, *et al*, "Plasma Glucose Responses to Glucose, Sucrose, and Honey in Patients with Diabetes Mellitus: An Analysis of Glycaemic and Peak Incremental Indices." Diabet Med 1985 Sep; 2(5): 371-373.

[50] Milligrams percent, or mg%, measures the number of milligrams of a given chemical or compound in 100 milliliters of blood.

[51] *Ibid.*, O Erejuwa, *et al*, "Oligosaccharides Might Contribute to the Anti-diabetic Effect of Honey: A Literature Review."

[52] A prebiotic is defined as "a selectively fermented ingredient that results in specific changes in the composition and/or activity of one or a limited number of the gastrointestinal microbiota, thus conferring benefit(s) upon host health." GR Gibson, *et al*, *J Nutr* (1995) and *J Food Sci Techol* (2010).

[53] For a calculation of the liver glycogen yield following the consumption of over 150 foods, the reader is directed to *Feed Your Brain First, The Honey Revolution*

Series – Part 3, TGBTGBooks.com, LLC and Xulon Press (2013).

Unmasking the Pretenders: the Facts About Artificial Sweeteners

[54] These include saccharin, cyclamate (Sweet'N Low® in Canada), aspartame (Equal or NutraSweet), acesulfame potassium (Sunett, Sweet One), sucralose (Splenda), neotame (NutraSweet), and stevia.

[55] R Dhingra, MD, *et al*, "Soft Drink Consumption and Risk of Developing Cardiometabolic Risk Factors and the Metabolic Syndrome in Middle-Aged Adults in the Community." *Circulation AHA* July 31, 2007; 480-488.

[56] DS Ludwig, *et al*, "Relation Between Consumption of Sugar-sweetened Drinks and Childhood Obesity: a Prospective, Observational Analysis." *Lancet* (2001) 357: 505-508.

[57] MB Schulze, *et al*, "Sugar-sweetened Beverages, Weight Gain, and Incidence of Type 2 Diabetes in Young and Middle-aged Women." *JAMA* (2004) 292: 927-934.

[58] *Ibid*.

Honey: Nature's Amazing Medicine

[59] This is not to say that any of these approaches is less valid than traditional medicine, but rather to say that I do not know much about any of these disciplines.

[60] Observational studies may not be controlled or randomized, that is to say, the intervention or "treatment" is not compared with a placebo or no treatment. It is difficult to assign a statistically valid association between an observation provided by some intervention and an outcome in these studies. Observational studies can, however, indicate trends or potential effects of some intervention.

At the least, observational studies emphasize the importance of conducting more clinical and controlled studies. [61] The clinical term for this process is *apoptosis*. The mechanisms of action for this phenomenon are varied, but may relate to the fact that honey improves cellular metabolism and energy production.

Honey for Weight Gain and Obesity

[62] L Chepulis and N Starkey, "The Long–term Effects of Feeding Honey Compared with Sucrose and a Sugar-free Diet on Weight Gain, Lipid Profiles, and DEXA Measurements in Rats." *Journal of Food Science* (2008) 73 (1) H1-H7.

[63] Al-Waili, *et al*, "Honey and Cardiovascular Risk Factors, in Normal Individuals and in Patients with Diabetes Mellitus or Dyslipidemia." *J Med Food* 2013 Dec; 16(12): 1063-78.

[64] N Yaghoobi, *et al*, "Natural Honey and Cardiovascular Risk Factors: Effects on Blood Glucose, Cholesterol, Triglycerides, CRP, and Body Weight Compared with Sucrose." *Scientific World Journal,* April 20, 2008; 8: 463-9.

Honey for Diabetes

[65] P Shambaugh, *et al*, "Differential Effects of Honey, Sucrose and Fructose on Blood Sugar Levels." *J Manipulative Physiol Ther* (1990) 13: 322-325.

[66] *Ibid*, Al-Waili, *et al.*

[67] GBKS Prasad, *et al*, "Subjects with Impaired Glucose Intolerance Exhibit a High Degree of Tolerance to Honey." *Journal of Medicinal Food* 10(3) 2007: 473-478.

[68] NF Sheard, *et al*, "Dietary Carbohydrate (Amount and Type) in the Prevention and Management of Diabetes." *Diabetes Care* 2004; 27:2266-2271.

[69] OO Erejuwa, *et al*, "Honey–a Novel Antidiabetic Agent." *Int J Biol Sci* 2012; 8(6): 913-34.

[70] M Abdulrhman, *et al*, "Metabolic Effects of Honey in Type 1 Diabetes Mellitus: a Randomized Crossover Pilot Study." *J Med Food* 2013 Jan; 16(1): 66-72.

[71] M Abdulrhman, *et al*, "Effects of Honey, Sucrose and Glucose on Blood Glucose and C-peptide in Patients with Type 1 Diabetes Mellitus." *Complement Ther Clin Pract* 2013 Feb; 19(1): 15-9.

[72] These metabolites are called advanced glycation end-products (AGEs), the same metabolites that are produced from intracellular oxidative stress due to hyperglycemia in patients with diabetes. AGEs can also be produced simply by heating sugars with fats or proteins (as in cooking). AGEs may also be formed inside the body through normal metabolism and aging. In hyperglycemia or diabetes, AGE formation can be increased beyond normal levels by oxidative stress.

[73] T Koschinsky, *et al*, "Orally absorbed reactive glycation products (glycotoxins): An environmental risk factor in diabetic nephropathy." *Medical Sciences* Vol. 94, 6474–6479, June 1997. From the Proceedings of the National Academy of Sciences USA.

[74] MH Dominiczak, "Obesity, Glucose Intolerance and Diabetes and Their Links to Cardiovascular Disease. Implications for Laboratory Medicine." *Clin Chem Lab Med* (2003) 41 (9): 1266–78.

[75] M Brownlee, "The Pathophysiology of Diabetic Complications: a Unifying Mechanism," *Diabetes* (2005) 54 (6): 1615–25.

[76] A Riboulet-Chavey, *et al*, "Methylglyoxal Impairs the Insulin Signaling Pathways Independently of the

Formation of Intracellular Reactive Oxygen Species." *Diabetes* Vol. 55, May 2006.

Honey for Cardiovascular Disease

[77] *Ibid*, N Al-Waili, *et al.*

[78] JM Alvarez-Suarez, *et al*, "Honey as a Source of Dietary Antioxidants: Structures, Bioavailability and Evidence of Protective Effects Against Human Chronic Diseases." *Curr Med Chem* 2013; 20(5): 621-638.

[79] *Ibid*, N Yaghoobi, *et al.*

[80] MK Rakha, *et al*, "Cardioactive and Vasoactive Effects of Natural Wild Honey against Cardiac Malperformance Induced by Hyperadrenergic Activity." *J Med Food* Mar 2008; 11 (1): 91-98.

[81] NS Al-Waili, MD, and NS Boni, "Natural Honey Lowers Plasma Prostaglandin Concentrations in Normal Individuals." *J Med Food*, 2003; 6(2): 129-33.

[82] HCY accumulation is also associated with osteoporosis and Alzheimer's disease, other diseases due to intracellular oxidative damage.

[83] SC El-Salch, "Honey Protects Against Homocysteine Elevation in Rats." *Vascular Disease Prevention*, Vol 3, No 4, November 2006, 313-318 (6).

Honey for the Brain

[84] *Feed Your Brain First*, TGBTGBooks.com, LLC (2013)

[85] Proteins from all kinds of meats (fish and seafood, beef, chicken, lamb) also contribute to brain fuel, but first the proteins must be broken down into amino acids, which then can produce glycogen in the liver. This process may take two to four hours after ingestion. Typical amounts of liver glycogen produced from proteins are calculated in *Feed Your Brain First*, TGBTGBooks.com, LLC (2013).

[86] The liver is the primary organ in the body that contains the fructose enzyme, fructokinase. Fructokinase in the liver starts the process whereby fructose is converted to and stored as liver glycogen. Furthermore, fructose, when ingested in the correct ratio with glucose, improves glucose uptake into the liver by acting to liberate the glucose enzyme (glucokinase) from the liver cell nucleus. Glucokinase is necessary for glucose to be converted to and stored as glycogen. Thus fructose is responsible for the creation and storage of glycogen in the liver that serves as the primary energy reserve for the brain.

[87] MB Vos, MD, MSPH, "Dietary Fructose Consumption Among US Children and Adults: The Third National Health and Nutrition Examination Survey." (2008)

[88] SW Rizkalla, "Health Implications of Fructose Consumption: A Review of Recent Data." *Nutrition & Metabolism* 2010, 7: 82

[89] D Jalal, MD, *et al*, "Increased Fructose Associates with Elevated Blood Pressure." 2010 Sept; 21(9): 1543-9.

[90] JS White, "Challenging the Fructose Hypothesis: New Perspectives on Fructose Consumption and Metabolism." (2013) American Society for Nutrition.

[91] Matthew 23: 24, New International Version

Honey for Menopause and Infertility

[92] J Lado-Abael, *et al*, "Menstrual Abnormalities in Women with Cushing's Disease Are Correlated with Hypercortisolemia Rather Than Raised Androgen Levels." *The Journal Endocrinology & Metabolism,* Vol 83, No 9: 3083-3088.

[93] Ed Kirby, *et al*, "Stress Increases Putative Gonadotrophin Inhibitory Hormone and Decreases Luteinizing Hormone in Male Rats." *Proc Natl Acad Sci USA* July 7, 2009; 106(27): 1132-9.

[94] JP Brown, *et al*, "Relations Among Menopausal Symptoms, Sleep Disturbance and Depressive Symptoms in Midlife." *Maturitas* Feb 20, 2009; 62(2): 184-9.

[95] V Tantrakul, and C Guilleminault, "Chronic sleep complaints in premenopausal women and their association with sleep-disordered breathing." *Lung* Mar-Apr 2009; 187(2): 82-92.

Honey for Gastrointestinal Health

[96] The definition of a probiotic is "live micro-organisms which, when administered in adequate amounts, confers a health benefit on the host." (From Jorgen Schlundt, " Health and Nutritional Properties of Probiotics in Food Including Powder Milk with Live Lactic Acid Bacteria." The World Health Organization, December 17, 2012.) This definition, although widely adopted, is not acceptable in the EU because it embeds a health claim which is not measurable according to GT Rijkers, *et al*, "Health Benefits and Health Claims of Probiotics: Bridging Science and Marketing." *British Journal of Nutrition* (2011) **106** (9): 1291–6.

[97] T Olofsson, PhD and A Vasquez, PhD, "Lactic Acid Bacteria – the Missing Link in Honey's Enigma." Unpublished study delivered at the First International Symposium on Honey and Human Health, Sacramento, CA, January 2008.

[98] The HYMN cycle refers to a term used by Mike McInnes in his presentation to the First International Symposium on Honey and Health held in Sacramento, CA in 2008. The acronym comes from the HoneY-MelatoniN Cycle described on a scientific poster presented at the Symposium and reprinted in *The Honey Revolution – Restoring the Health of Future Generations*, WorldClassEmprise, LLC, 2008.

[99] D Bandyopadhlyay, *et al*, "Involvement of Reactive Oxygen Species in Gastric Ulceration: Protection by Melatonin." ***Indian J Exp Biol***, June 2002; 40(6): 693-705.

Honey for Thyroid Conditions

[100] L Xia, *et al*, "Alterations in Hypothalamus-Pituitary-Adrenal/Thyroid Axes and Gonadotropin-releasing Hormone in the Patients with Primary Insomnia: a Clinical Research." Published online August 9, 2013.

[101] M Maggio, *et al*, "Stress Hormones, Sleep Deprivation and Cognition in Older Adults." ***Maturitas*** 2013 Sep; 76(1): 22-44.

[102] G Copinschi and A Caufriez, "Sleep and Hormonal Changes in Aging." ***Endocrinol Metab Clin North Am*** 2013 Jun; 42(2): 371-89.

[103] SM Schmid, *et al*, "Partial Sleep Restriction Modulates Secretory Activity of Thyrotropic Axis in Healthy Men." ***J Sleep Res*** Apr 2013; 22(2): 166-9.

[104] PV Krishnan, *et al*, "Prevalence of sleep abnormalities and their association among hypothyroid patients in an Indian population." ***Sleep Med*** Dec 2012; 13(10): 1232-7.

Honey for Depression

[105] F Duval, *et al*, "Cortisol Hypersecretion in Unipolar Major Depression with Melancholic and Psychotic Features: Dopaminergic, Noradrenergic and Thyroid Correlates." ***Psychoneuroendocrinology*** 2006 Aug; 31(7): 876-88.

[106] DA Axelson, *et al*, "Hypercortisolaemia and Hippocampal Changes in Depression." ***Psychiat Res*** (1993) 47: 163-73.

[107] Dinan TG, "Glucocorticoids and the Genesis of Depressive Illness: A Psychobiological Model." *Br J Psychiatry* (1994) 164: 365-71.

[108] JF Lopez, *et al*, "Regulation of 5HT1a Receptor, Glucocorticoid and Mineralocorticoid Receptor in Rat and Human Hippocampus: Implications for the Neurobiology of Depression." **Biol Psychiatry** (1998) 43: 547-573

[109] SC Yudofsky and RE Hales, *The American Psychiatric Publishing Textbook of Neuropsychiatry and Behavioral Neurosciences*, 5th (2007) American Psychiatric Pub, Inc.

[110] *Ibid*, Axelson.

[111] *Ibid*, Dinan.

The Benefits of Honey for Sleep

[112] M Hyman, MD, *Ultrametabolism,* Scribner (2006) and *The Ultrametabolism Cookbook*, Scribner (2007).

[113] D Johnson, MD, "Fractured Sleep Exacts a Heavy Toll." *Medscape* February 19, 2014.

Honey and Dreams

[114] H Marshall, Mölle & Born, 2006

[115] MA Tucker, *et al*, "A Daytime Nap Containing Solely non-REM Sleep Enhances Declarative but not Procedural Memory." *Neurobiology of Learning and Memory* (2006) **86** (2): 241–7.

[116] JM Siegel, "The REM Sleep-Memory Consolidation Hypothesis."

[117] G Mitchison and F Crick, "The Function of Dream Sleep." *Nature* (1983) 304 (5922): 111–14.

[118] Morrissey, Duntley & Anch, 2004.

[119] E Bruel-Jungerman, *et al*, "Adult Hippocampal Neurogenesis, Synaptic Plasticity and Memory: Facts and Hypotheses." *Rev Neurosci* (2006) **18** (2): 93–114.

[120] T Endo, *et al*, "Selective REM Sleep Deprivation in Humans: Effects on Sleep and Sleep EEG." *The American Journal of Physiology* (1998) **274** (4 Pt 2): R1186–R1194.

Honey for Memory and Learning

[121] SR Bodnoff, *et al*, "Enduring Effects of Chronic Corticosterone Treatment on Spatial Learning, Synaptic Plasticity, and Hippocampal Neuropathology in Young and mid-aged Rats." *J Neurosci* (1995) 15, 61-69.

[122] CD Conrad, *et al*, "Chronic Stress Impairs Rat Spatial Memory on the Y Maze, and This Effect is Blocked by Tianeptine Pretreatment." *Behav Neurosci*, 1996, 110, 1321-1334.

[123] VN Luine, *et al*, "Effects of Chronic Corticosterone Ingestion on Spatial Memory Performance and Hippocampal Serotonergic Function." *Brain Res* (1993) 616, 65-70.

[124] VN Luine, *et al*, "Repeated Stress Causes Reversible Impairments of Spatial Memory Performance." **Brain Res** (1994), 639, 167-170.

[125] M Mauri, et al, "Memory Impairment in Cushing's Disease." *Acta Neurol Scand* (1993) 87, 52-55.

[126] MN Starkman, "Hippocampal Formation Volume, Memory Dysfunction, and Cortisol Levels in Patients with Cushing's Syndrome." (1992) *Biol Psychiatry* 32, 756-765.

[127] S Sharma, MD, FCCP and R Franco, MD, FCCP, "Sleep and Its Disorders in Pregnancy." *Wisconsin Medical Journal*, 2004 Volume 103, No 5.

[128] JW Newcomer, *et al*, "Glucocorticoid-induced Impairment in Declarative Memory Performance in Adult Humans." *J Neurosci* (1994) 14, 2047-2053.

[129] *Ibid*, M Mauri, *et al*.

[130] LM Chepulis, NJ Starkey, *et al*, "The Effects of Longterm Honey, Sucrose or Sugar-free Diets on Memory and Anxiety in Rats." *Physiol Behav* 2009 Jun 22; 97(3-4):359-68.

[131] AJ Graveling, *et al*, "Acute Hypoglycemia Impairs Executive Cognitive Function in Adults with and without Type 1 Diabetes." *Diabetes Care* 2013 Oct; 36(10): 3240-6.

[132] SK Dash, "Cognitive Impairment and Diabetes." *Recent Pat Endocr Metab Immune Drug Discov* 2013 May; 7(2): 155-65.

[133] SJ Won, *et al*, "Recurrent/Moderate Hypoglycemia Induces Hippocampal Dendritic Injury, Microglial Activation, and Cognitive Impairment in Diabetic Rats." *J Neuroinflammation* 2012 Jul 25; 9:182.

[134] C Enzinger, *et al*, "Risk Factors for Progression of Brain Atrophy in Aging." *Neurology* (2005) 64: 1704-1711.

[135] PK Crane, *et al*, "Glucose Levels and Risk of Dementia." *New England J Med* (2013) 369: 540-548.

[136] RO Roberts, *et al*, "Relative Intake of Macronutrients Impacts Risk of Mild Cognitive Impairment or Dementia." *J Alzheimers Dis* (2012) 32: 329-339.

Honey and Alzheimer's Disease

[137] Alzheimer's Association 2013 Alzheimer's Disease Facts and Figures, www.alz.org.

[138] H Mahboobi, *et al*, "Humanin: A Possible Linkage between Alzheimer's Disease and Type 2 Diabetes." *CNS Neurol Disord Drug Targets* (2013) Dec 22 [Epub ahead of print].

[139] *Ibid.*

[140] J Bloemer, *et al*, "Impaired insulin signaling and mechanisms of memory loss." *Prog Mol Biol Transl Sci* (2014) 121: 413-49.

[141] AS Lim, *et al*, "Sleep Fragmentation and the Risk of Incident Alzheimer's Disease and Cognitive Decline in Older Persons." *Sleep* (2013) Jul 1; 36(7): 1027-1032.

142 G Hurtado-Alvarado, *et al*, " Sleep Loss As a Factor to Induce Cellular and Molecular Inflammatory Variations." *Clin Dev Immunol* [Epub 2013 Dec 3].
143 *Ibid*.

Honey for Hypertension

144 James E. Gangwisch, *et al*, "Short Sleep Duration as a Risk Factor for Hypertension: Analyses of the First National Health and Nutrition Examination Survey," *Hypertension* 2006; 47: 833-839.

The Effects of Honey on the Immune System

145 J Zidan, *et al*, "Prevention of Chemotherapy-induced Neutropenia by Special Honey Intake." *Medical Oncology* (2006) Vol 23, No 4, 549-552. First published in *American Journal of Clinical Nutrition* (1998), Vol 67, 519S-526S.
146 N Al-Waili, MD, "Effect of Honey on Antibody Production Against Thymus-Dependent and Thymus-Independent Antigens in Primary and Secondary Immune Responses." *Journal of Medicinal Foods* 7 (4) 2004, 492–495.
147 N Al-Waili, MD, PhD, "Short Communication–Effects of Daily Consumption of Honey Solution on Hematological Indices and Blood Levels of Minerals and Enzymes in Normal Individuals." *Journal of Medicinal Foods* (2003) Vol 6, No 2.

Honey and Cancer

148 Data from the World Health Organization, 2013.
149 *Ibid*, N Al-Waili, MD.
150 *Ibid*, N Al-Waili, MD, PhD, "Short Communication–Effects of Daily Consumption of Honey Solution on

Hematological Indices and Blood Levels of Minerals and Enzymes in Normal Individuals."

[151] WY Attia, *et al*, "The Anti-tumor Effect of Bee Honey in Ehrlich Ascite Tumor Model of Mice Is Coincided with Stimulation of the Immune Cells." *The Egyptian Journal of Immunology* (2008) Vol 15, No 2, pp 169-183.

[152] N Abuharfeil, *et al*, The Effect of Bee Honey on the Proliferation Activity of Human B- and T-Lymphocytes and the Activity of Phagocytes." *Food and Agricultural Immunology* (1999) Vol II, No 2, pp 169-177.

[153] M Viuda-Martos, *et al*, "Functional Properties of Honey, Propolis, and Royal Jelly." *Journal of Food Science*, (2008) Vol 73, No 9, pp R117-R124.

[154] AN Fauzi, *et al*, "Tualang Honey Induces Apoptosis and Disrupts the Mitochondrial Membrane Potential of Human Breast and Cervical Cancer Cell Lines." *Food and Chemical Toxicology* (2001) Vol 1, No 4, pp 871-878.

[155] SK Jaganathan and M Mandal, "Honey constituents and Their Apoptotic Effect in Colon Cancer Cells." *Journal of ApiProduct and ApiMedical Science* (2009) Vol 1, No 2, pp 29-36.

[156] S Samarghandian, *et al*, "Honey Induces Apoptosis in Renal Cell Carcinoma." *Pharmacognosy Magazine* (2011) Vol 7, No 25, pp 46-52.

[157] HX Wang, *et al*, " Antimutagenic Effect of Various Honeys and Sugars Against Trp-p-1." *Journal of Agricultural and Food Chemistry* (2002) Vol 50, No 23, pp 6923-6928.

[158] S Saxena, *et al*, "Suppression of Error Prone Pathway Is Responsible for Antimutagenic Activity of Honey." *Food and Chemical Toxicology* (2012) Vol 50, No 3-4, pp 625-633.

[159] R Tomassin, *et al*, "Oral Administration of *Aloe vera* and Honey Reduces Walker Tumor Growth by Decreasing Cell

Proliferation and Increasing Apoptosis in Tumor Tissue." *Phytotherapy Research* (2011) Vol 25, No 4, pp 619-623.

[160] *Ibid*, AN Fauzi, *et al*.

[161] E Pichichero, *et al*, "Acacia Honey and Chrysin Reduce Proliferation of Melanoma Cells through Alterations in Cell Cycle Progression." *International Journal of Oncology* (2010) Vol 37, N 4, pp 973-981.

The Antimicrobial Benefits of Honey

[162] Quoted from *Honey The Gourmet Medicine* by Joe Traynor, Kovak Books 2002, page 5.

[163] *Ibid*.

[164] *Ibid*.

[165] T Henle, *et al*, "Identification and Quantification of Methylglyoxal as the Dominant Antibacterial Constituent of Manuka (*Leptospermum scoparium*) Honeys from New Zealand." *Molecular Nutrition and Food Research* 2008 April; 52(4): 483-9.

[166] ZH Israili, "Antimicrobial Properties of Honey." *Am J Ther* 2013 June 18.

[167] S Blair, PhD, Unpublished data presented by the author at the First International Symposium on Honey and Human Health, Sacramento, CA (January 2008).

[168] S Blair, *et al*, "The Effect of Standard Heat and Filtration Processing Procedures on Antimicrobial Activity and Hydrogen Peroxide Levels in Honey." *Front Microbiol* 2012 Jul 27; 3: 265.

[169] *Ibid*, ZH Israili.

Honey and Wound Care

[170] *Ibid*, Traynor.

[171] N Al-Waili, "Honey for Wound Healing, Ulcers, and Burns; Data Supporting Its Use in Clinical Practice." *Scientific World Journal* Apr 5 2011; 11: 766-87.

[172] J Majtan, *et al*, "Anti-biofilm Effects of Honey Against Wound Pathogens *P. mirabilis* and *E. cloacae.*" *Phytother Res* Jan 28 2014; 28 (1): 69-75.

Honey for Oral Health, Gingivitis, and Periodontal Disease

[173] FR Khan, *et al*, "Honey: Nutritional and Medicinal value." *Int J Clin Pract* (2007) Oct; 61(10): 1705-7.

[174] PC Molan, "The Potential of Honey to Promote Oral Wellness." *Gen Dent* (2001) Nov-Dec; 49(6): 584-9.

[175] PC Molan, *et al*, "The Effects of Manuka Honey on Plaque and Gingivitis: a Pilot Study." *J Int Acad Periodontol* (2004) Apr; 6(2): 63-7.

[176] S Aparna, *et al*, "A Comparative Evaluation of the Antibacterial Efficacy of Honey in Vitro and Antiplaque Efficacy in a 4-day Plaque Regrowth Model in Vivo: Preliminary Results. *J Periodontol* (2012) Sep; 83(9): 1116-21.

The Miscellaneous Benefits of Consuming Honey

[177] *Ibid*, IM Paul, MD, *et al*.

Honey: the Super Fuel for Exercise

[178] Fats do not under any circumstances contribute to glucose formation or to storage of glucose as glycogen in human metabolism.

[179] For more meal selection options designed to fill the liver glycogen tank at every meal and snack, please

see the recipe and menu planner section of *Feed Your Brain First*.

180 *Sport Nutrition for Health and Performance* by Melinda Manore, Arizona State University and Janice Thomson, University of New Mexico, Publisher, Human Kinetics, Champaign, IL (2000) p. 43.

Honey for Alcohol Detoxification and Liver Health

181 HP Rang and MM Dale, "Fructose Recycling of NAD from NADH." *Pharmacology* Churchill Livingstone 1991, Edinburgh Chapter 39, pp 890-891.
182 NS Al-Waili, "Effects of Daily Consumption of Honey Solution on Haematological Indices and Blood Levels of Minerals and Enzymes in Normal Individuals." *Journal of Medicinal Food* (2006) Vol 6, No 2.
183 NS Al-Waili, *et al*, "Influence of Various Diet Regimes on Deterioration of Hepatic Function and Haematalogical Parameters Following Carbon Tetrachloride: a Potential Role of Natural Honey." *Nat Prod Res* (2006) Nov; 20(13): 1258-1264.

Honey and Infants

184 MG Tanzi and MP Gabay, "Association between honey consumption and infant botulism." *Pharmacotherapy* (2002) Nov; 22(11): 1479-83.
185 JS Spika, *et al*, "Risk Factors for Infant Botulism in the United States." *Am J Dis Child* (1989) Jul; 143(7): 828-32.

Honey: the All-star Super Food

186 This statement simply indicates that the studies on which this book's health benefits are derived have been

based exclusively on the consumption of raw, unfiltered honey. It is not meant to imply that the processed honey packed and sold under several well-known brand names is bad for you.

ABOUT THE AUTHOR

R on Fessenden, MD, MPH, is a retired medical doctor. He received his MD from the University of Kansas School of Medicine in 1970 and his Masters in Public Health from the University of Hawaii School of Public Health in 1982.

For the past six years, Dr. Fessenden has been researching and writing about the health benefits of consuming honey. He has spoken at numerous venues across the United States and Canada about this topic, including a presentation entitled, "Living Healthier–Aging Well with Honey" delivered at the Excellence in Aging Care Symposium in Fredericton, New Brunswick in 2012 and in 2014.

His previous published works include:

The Honey Revolution – Restoring the Health of Future Generations, WorldClassEmprise, LLC (2008) by Ron Fessenden, MD, MPH and Mike McInnes, MRPS.

The Honey Revolution – Abridged, WorldClassEmprise, LLC (2010) by Ron Fessenden, MD, MPH and Mike McInnes, MRPS.

Feed Your Brain First, The Honey Revolution Series – Part 3, TGBTGBooks.com, LLC (2013) by Ronald E Fessenden, MD, MPH

For more information go to:

www.tgbtgbooks.com
or email Dr. Fessenden at
ron@tgbtgbooks.com